DogsTrust

LIVING WITH A

Rescued Dog

Julia Barnes

RINGPRESS

THE QUESTION OF GENDER
The 'he' pronoun is used throughout this book in favour of the rather impersonal 'it', but no gender bias is intended at all.

ACKNOWLEDGEMENTS
Thanks to Vicki Horsley for her important contributions to the text; to Dogs Trust Veterinary Director Chris Laurence QVRM, TD, BVSc, MRCVS for the health care information in Chapter Nine; and to Jo Bird, Diane Clark, Paul and Mandy Smith, Tracey Rae, Sharon Beer, Carol Shreeve, Fred and Peggy Henney, and Simon Round for sharing their personal experiences with rescued dogs. Finally, thanks to the staff at Dogs Trust rehoming centres for their help and co-operation with this project.

Published by Ringpress Books Ltd,
A division of Interpet Publishing,
Vincent Lane, Dorking, Surrey, RH4 3YX

Designed by Sarah Williams.

First Published 2004
© 2004 RINGPRESS BOOKS

ISBN 1 86054 224 7

Printed and bound in China

0 9 8 7 6 5 4 3 2 1

CONTENTS

FOREWORD

Photo by Paul Keevil/Dogs Today.

If you are reading this book, it is because you are interested in sharing your life with a rescued dog. Congratulations! You have already taken the first step towards finding the dog of your dreams.

There is a rescued dog to suit almost every owner and lifestyle – at Dogs Trust, the UK's largest dog charity, we look after more than 11,500 dogs each year, so we are bound to have the perfect dog for you.

Many people make the mistake of thinking that there is something wrong with a rescued dog, but the vast majority of dogs find themselves looking for a new home through no fault of their own. Marriage break-ups, a baby in the family, or allergies are just some of the reasons given by owners.

In *Living With a Rescued Dog*, we prepare you for what life will really be like with your new companion. As well as detailed information on choosing the right dog, you will find in these pages advice on caring for and training a dog throughout his life. There is much to gain from other people's experiences, and we feature many real-life case histories, where owners tell their own personal accounts of giving a dog a second chance.

What is clear from reading these case studies is that the relationship between people and dogs is unique – and the bond between a rescued dog and his human family is extra special. Giving a

dog the chance of a happy, loving future, and earning his trust and love, is one of the most rewarding relationships you can ever have.

If, after reading the book, and having carefully considered your circumstances, you are more eager than ever, then contact your nearest Dogs Trust centre – we'll be happy to hear from you!

Clarissa Baldwin

Clarissa Baldwin
Chief Executive, Dogs Trust

CHAPTER ONE

CHOOSING A RESCUED DOG

T he decision to take on a dog is a major undertaking, which will have a big impact on your life. If you opt for a puppy, you will have all the fun of watching your dog grow and develop – but there is no escaping the fact that it is hard work for the first 12 months or so. If you decide to take on an adult rescued dog, you will face a challenge of a different kind. In most cases, you will be adopting a dog who has lost his home and the only people he has ever known. Hopefully, this will be the start of a great new life together – but as with every big decision you take, it is important to weigh up the pros and the cons before you go ahead.

DOGS IN RESCUE

There are many reasons why a dog needs to be rehomed. Among the most common reasons are:

- **Change of circumstance:** This could mean a change in employment so no one is at home to look after a dog, or a move to a house or a flat where dogs are not allowed.
- **Partnership splitting up:** When a relationship comes to an end, the dog often has no home to go to.
- **Starting a family:** Sadly, a couple who decide to start a family may decide they no longer want a dog.
- **Death or illness:** A dog may lose his home if his elderly owner has to go into residential care, or if his owner dies.
- **Strays:** These are the dogs found wandering on the streets whose owners cannot be traced.
- **Ex-racing Greyhounds:** Racing Greyhounds who have retired are in need of new homes.
- **Puppies:** Puppies may be bought in for rehoming if a family pet has had a litter. A stray may be found with a litter, or pups may be found abandoned. Sometimes a bitch is pregnant when she arrives for rehoming, and puppies are born at the centre.
- **Neglect:** There are some dogs up for adoption following a history of being neglected or cruelly treated by their owners.

THE CHARITIES

The need to find many thousands of new homes every year for rescued dogs means that both the old, established charities and many newer organisations are working at full stretch. There are differences in the size of the charities, and the work they do, which may influence which organisation you approach. The charities work closely with each other, united in the task of providing a new future for homeless dogs.

DOGS TRUST

On average, Dogs Trust cares for around 11,500 dogs a year. New homes are found for around 9,500 dogs, and a small proportion – perhaps around 500 – will be reunited with their original owners. Dogs Trust has a 'non destruct' policy, which means that a dog is never needlessly put to sleep. Dogs Trust has 15 rehoming centres, a Sanctuary for dogs who will socialise with other dogs but are unsuitable for rehoming, and a

Dogs Trust find homes for a total of 9,500 dogs every year.

special home for older dogs. All dogs are temperament-tested, vaccinated, neutered and microchipped before being rehomed.

BATTERSEA DOGS' HOME

The famous London rehoming centre is as busy as ever – there may be as many as 500 dogs there at any one time. In addition, Battersea has two rural rehoming centres in the south of England. These centres provide a better environment for bigger dogs, as well as enlarging the catchment area of people looking for dogs. On average, Battersea rehomes over 4,000 dogs a year. Each dog is temperament-tested, vaccinated, neutered, and microchipped before being rehomed.

RSPCA

The RSPCA works with all types of animals, and, on average 70,000 animals are rehomed a year. In many cases, the animals are unwanted or abandoned. RSPCA inspectors also investigate cases of cruelty. All dogs rehomed by the RSPCA are vaccinated, neutered and microchipped before adoption.

BLUE CROSS

This charity has eight rehoming centres, and homes are found for around 2,000 dogs a year. On average, dogs stay in the centres for a month before rehoming. Every dog is temperament-tested, vaccinated, neutered and microchipped before adoption.

WOOD GREEN ANIMAL SHELTER

There are three shelters based in the south-east of England, and between them they take in

6,000 animals, which include dogs, cats, field animals (horses, donkeys, goats etc.), and small animals (rabbits, guinea pigs etc.). On average 1,500 dogs are rehomed each year.

RETIRED GREYHOUND TRUST
Finding homes for former racing Greyhounds is a major concern, and there are a number of charities that concentrate on Greyhound rescue, or Greyhound and Lurcher rescue. The biggest charity for rehoming ex-racers in the UK is the Retired Greyhound Trust. At any one time, the Trust will have around 750 Greyhounds in its care – usually placed in third-party kennels and paid for by the Trust. The number of Greyhounds that are rehomed in a year stands at just over 2,600. All Greyhounds are health-checked and neutered before being rehomed.

BREED RESCUE
There are a number of organisations who concentrate on rehoming one breed only. These are usually associated with specialist breed clubs, which are affiliated with the national Kennel Club. They are generally run by dedicated volunteers. If you have decided you want to adopt a particular breed, contact the Kennel Club, who will put you in touch with the relevant breed society.

TAKING ON A RESCUED DOG
Given the fact that so many dogs need rehoming, it would be logical to assume that the charities are crying out for people who will take the dogs off their hands. However, it is in the interests of the charity concerned – and most particularly, of the dog involved – that the

Many Greyhounds who have retired from racing need new homes.

rehoming is a success. It is therefore important to examine your motives for wanting to take on a rescued dog.

"I feel sorry for dogs that have been ill-treated."
It is laudable to want to help dogs who have fallen on hard times, but this reason is not enough on its own. You must be aware of the care and training that may be involved, and work out if you can provide it.

"I am an experienced dog owner, and I am ready to work at the problems that may be associated with rehoming an adult."
This would-be owner is ideal – not only are they used to dogs, they have an understanding of the work and commitment needed to rehome an older pet.

"I would like to give a dog a second chance, even though I know it may be hard work initially."

Weigh up the pros and the cons before taking on a rescued dog.

Every chance of success here, as the would-be owner is being realistic about possible problems that may lie ahead.

"I have taken on rescued dogs before, and I understand what is involved."
No problems in this case. There are some people who have a lifelong commitment to caring for rescued dogs, and they are ready to devote themselves to giving these dogs a second chance.

THE CHALLENGE

People who successfully rehome rescued dogs derive a huge amount of satisfaction from the work they do. They know they have given a dog a fresh start, possibly helped the dog to overcome behavioural problems caused by his difficult start in life, and they are rewarded with

a loving and affectionate companion. For some owners, the sky's the limit, and they train their rescued dogs to become canine stars competing in Obedience, Agility or Working Trials (see pages 86-91).

These success stories are not few and far between. Dogs are amazingly adaptable animals, and most will put all their troubles behind them if they are given the help and support they need to settle into a new life. The key element is to find a dog who will suit your own particular lifestyle so that you can meet his needs and he has every chance of fitting in with you and your family.

CHOOSING A BREED

There are nearly 200 pedigree breeds registered with the English Kennel Club, and theoretically, you could find any of these breeds in a rehoming charity. In fact, it is rare to find the highly expensive and exotic breeds, as they are unlikely to be discarded. However, the bigger charities will usually have a reasonable cross-section of different breeds.

The Kennel Club divides breeds into seven groups, and the dogs within each group share certain characteristics. It is important to find out as much as possible about a breed, as this will give you an indication of the dog's temperament, trainability, grooming and exercise requirements.

At rehoming centres, many of the dogs will be cross-breeds, but they will often bear a strong resemblance to one of their parents. However, remember that each dog is an individual and it can be unwise to rely too much on breed type to assess character.

TOY

The dogs in this group are the miniatures of the canine world. They are the little lap dogs who were bred to be companions rather than working dogs. The biggest in the group is the Cavalier King Charles Spaniel, and the smallest is the Chihuahua, which is the smallest dog breed in the world.

These dogs do not need very much exercise, but in most cases, they thrive on human companionship and will not be happy if they are left on their own for too long.

A number of breeds in this group, such as the Yorkie, the Maltese, and the Papillon, have glamorous long coats, which require the attention of a dedicated groomer. Toy dogs do come up for rehoming, often when an elderly owner can no longer look after their pet.

GUNDOGS

Bred to work as shooting companions, the dogs in this group are mostly strong and energetic. They are generally of medium size and weight, and they require plenty of exercise.

The retrieving breeds, which include the Labrador and the Golden Retriever, often make excellent family dogs. Most love to retrieve – or at least to have something in their mouth – and many find water irresistible. Retriever crosses are found in many rehoming centres.

The Spaniel breeds, which include the English Springer and the Cocker Spaniel, have long, feathered coats, which require considerable grooming. They were bred to flush out game, and when on a walk, they tend to be busy, with their nose to the ground and tail wagging.

Setters and Pointers were used to sight game and then to freeze on point. These noble-looking, sporting dogs need lots of exercise, but they also enjoy their creature comforts.

In Europe, all-round gundogs were bred, who could hunt, point and retrieve. The Weimaraner and the German Shorthaired Pointer have both become popular breeds in the UK.

TERRIERS

Terriers come in all shapes and sizes, ranging from the Airedale, the king of terriers, who measures around 59 cms (23 ins) at the shoulder, to the West Highland White Terrier, who measures around 28 cms (11 ins).

A Retriever cross, like this Labrador cross, often makes an excellent family companion.

Fred and Peggy Henney owned a Poodle for 16 years, and when their dog died, they said they would never get another. But they had not reckoned for their grand-daughter, Emma, who works at the Dogs Trust rehoming centre at Ilfracombe.

"I always said my Poodle could never be replaced," said Peggy. "We had him for 16 years, and we were completely tuned in to each other. I didn't even think about looking for another dog. But then a Shih Tzu called Suki came into the rehoming centre where Emma works, and she said we had to see him. Well, it didn't take long before we fell in love with him.

"We have a pedigree for Suki, and it appears as though his grandparents and parents were bred in the USA. He was owned by an elderly woman, and when she died, Suki was taken in by Dogs Trust. He was about three years old at the time.

"When he first came to us, he was very aloof. It seemed as though he didn't have any love to give. I don't think he was ever badly treated, but he had had a big upheaval in his life, and he was put out by it.

"When you get a puppy, you bond with him straight away, but when you take on an older dog, it takes longer. You have to get to know each other. It took Suki a little while to build up his trust. We just gave him lots of love, and waited for him to respond when he was ready. Now he's absolutely adorable. He sometimes sits on the floor and looks between my husband and me, and you can almost hear him thinking: I've fallen on my feet!'

"Suki has always been well behaved, and so we didn't need to train him. He's a very biddable dog. He loves going out to the shops, and he adores being in the car. He does enjoy exercise, but very much on his terms. If my husband takes him for a walk to the post office, it may be that Suki decides he doesn't want to go all the way!

"When he came to us, Suki was in full coat. With the help of Emma, I keep his legs clipped, and tidy up around his face. I also make sure the coat doesn't reach to the ground. He still looks very smart, but the coat is easier to maintain. I used to clip my Poodle, so between us, Emma and I can make quite a reasonable job of it. It certainly saves on trips to the grooming parlour.

"We have now had Suki for three years, and I really cannot imagine being without him. He really is the light of our lives."

Suki: It took time to build up trust.

Bull Terriers, like this one, have a devoted fan club.

Many of these breeds, such as the popular Jack Russell, were bred to go to earth after their quarry, and a lot of terriers have a feisty, spirited character.

The Bull Terrier and the Staffordshire Bull Terrier go back to the days when dogs were bred for fighting. Fortunately, these breeds have reinvented themselves, and are highly valued as family pets.

If you are attracted to terriers, you will find a wide range of small terrier types, and larger dogs, which are more like Staffordshire Bull Terriers, at most rehoming centres.

HOUNDS

Hounds can be divided into two categories: hounds who hunt by scent, and hounds who hunt by sight. Scenthounds include the Dachshund (the smallest breed in the group), the Beagle and the Basset Hound.

The sighthounds, which include the Greyhound and the Afghan Hound, are bred to run, and their physique is that of a finely tuned athlete. Despite their amazing speed, sighthounds do not require huge amounts of exercise, and they are more than happy to take life easy on the sofa. Greyhounds and Lurchers (which is the name given to any dog that is crossed with a sighthound) make up quite a large percentage of dogs that need rehoming.

WORKING

This group includes many of the canine heavyweights, such as the St. Bernard, the Newfoundland and the Mastiff. These impressive looking dogs are strong and powerful, and although they do not require strenuous exercise, they do need a lot to eat.

A number of the working breeds, such as the

Lurchers come in all shapes and sizes.

Rottweiler, the Dobermann and the Bullmastiff were originally bred to guard. This instinct may not be apparent in some dogs, but generally they benefit from being trained by an experienced handler. It is preferable if these breeds, or cross-breeds that come up for rehoming are adopted by someone who is used to handling big, powerful dogs.

PASTORAL

All the breeds in this group have a history of herding livestock. It includes the Collie breeds: the Rough and the Smooth, the Bearded and the Border. These breeds tend to have high energy requirements, but none more so than the Border Collie or Working Sheepdog, who are seemingly tireless. These highly intelligent dogs also need plenty of mental stimulation, and as a result they come up for rehoming when previous owners have not had the time to devote to them.

The German Shepherd Dog is generally thought of as a guard dog because it is the chosen breed of the police and security forces. In fact, the first German Shepherds were used to herd and protect flocks. German Shepherds and German Shepherd crosses make wonderful companions, but they often benefit if they go to someone who has experience of the breed.

UTILITY

The uniting factor within these breeds is that they don't fit into any other group! Breeds as diverse as the Dalmatian, the Bulldog and the Poodle are included, and they have absolutely nothing in common!

If you come across a breed or a cross-breed in this group, you will need to find out about its background, its temperament, and its exercise requirements before deciding whether it will fit into your lifestyle.

HEINZ 57

Sometimes a dog will bear no resemblance to a breed, and does not even fit into a breed type.

The energetic Border Collie or Working Sheepdog thrives on having plenty to do.

A litter of Heinz 57 pups – you can only guess at their parentage, and what size they will grow to.

Dogs such as these are known as mongrels or Heinz 57s! The parents (and probably the grandparents) of a Heinz 57 will be mongrels or mixed breeds, and the genetic make-up of the offspring is so muddled that no clear breed type emerges.

If you are planning to adopt a mongrel pup, you can only guess as to what size he will end up as once he is an adult!

DO YOUR HOMEWORK!

If you are planning to take on a rescued dog, do your homework first. Find out as much as you can about the breeds or breed types you are attracted to, and be honest with yourself about the home you have to offer. Remember, the average life expectancy of a dog is 13 years, and so you must be confident that you can offer a home for life.

CHAPTER TWO

THE PROCESS OF ADOPTION

Before you start your search for a rescued dog, it is important to consider the impact that a dog will have on your family.

FINANCIAL IMPLICATIONS

Most charities ask for a donation to help recoup some of their costs. This does not constitute a major investment, but you should be aware of the other costs involved in dog ownership. These will include:

- Food – the bigger the dog, the more he will eat.
- Routine health care (vaccination, worming treatment, flea protection).
- Grooming – if you adopt a dog with a coat that requires stripping or clipping, you will have to pay a professional groomer (see page ???).
- Vet bills – hopefully your dog will not have too many of these, but you need to be able to put your dog's welfare first at all times.
- Insurance – this is optional, but taking out a

policy will certainly give you peace of mind with regard to health care.

- Equipment – grooming gear, collar, lead, bowls, bed, etc. (see pages 33-36).
- Boarding kennels – a consideration if you like to go away for your holidays.
- Microchipping (or some other form of ID). It is a legal requirement for your dog to have a collar and tag. Ideally, this should be permanent, such as microchipping or a tattoo, plus an identity tag on the collar. A number of rehoming organisations microchip all dogs before they leave.
- Neutering – in many cases (such as at Dogs Trust), the rehoming charity ensures that all dogs are neutered before they leave. But if not, it may be a cost you have to meet. Many rescue organisations also issue vouchers that entitle you to a discount.

GIVING TIME

Be absolutely honest about the time you will be able to spend with your dog. If you are out at day away from home on a shopping trip, or going to a football match, unless you make arrangements for someone to look after your dog. If you plan to go away on holiday, you will have to find somewhere that will allow dogs, find a reputable boarding kennel, or employ an experienced house/dog-sitter.

Make sure you have the time to devote to owning a dog – particularly if you want to start with a puppy.

work all day, and there is no one at home, it would be better to choose a less demanding pet, such as a cat. Although some breed types need more training and mental stimulation than others, all dogs require quality time with their family.

Exercise requirements should be considered (rain or shine!), and if you are attracted by the long-haired breeds, you must allocate time for regular grooming sessions.

RESTRICTED FREEDOM

Constant companionship is one of the great pleasures of owning a dog, but 'constant' means just that. If you own a dog, you will have to consider his needs as well as your own, and this may mean compromising what you do. For example, you cannot plan to spend the whole

STILL KEEN?

If you remain undaunted by the impact that a dog will have on your lifestyle, you are now ready for the most exciting part – going to choose your new companion.

To find out about the different rescue organisations, try the following:

- Log on to the internet to find out where rehoming centres are located, as well as gathering information about the charity concerned.
- Make enquiries at your local veterinary practice. The vet will be in constant contact with rehoming organisations in the area.
- If you want a specific breed, contact the Kennel Club, which keeps a register of breed rescue organisations.

FIRST VISIT

When you first visit a rehoming centre, you must make a pledge not to let your heart rule your head. If you had your own way, you would probably take *all* the dogs home with you. Then there is the dog with the sad eyes or the funny ears that you cannot resist – and bang goes all your well-thought-out plans for the type of dog that would most suit your family.

The aim of all rescue organisations is to match dogs and owners so that there is the best possible chance of the new relationship working out well. The worst scenario for the dog – and for the charity – is for a dog to be returned within weeks of rehoming because the adopters have not been able to cope. This is deeply distressing for the dog, who has had to put up with yet more upset in his life, and it is also hard for the adopters, who feel a terrible sense of failure.

Be as realistic as possible about the type of home you can offer, and listen to the advice given by the rehoming organisation. The process of adoption will vary depending on which charity you approach. Do not be put off because you cannot rush home with a dog on day one; it is far better to take things slowly rather than to repent at leisure.

Dogs Trust has worked out a stage-by-stage adoption process, and although details may vary, the broad principles will be followed by all rehoming agencies.

ASKING QUESTIONS

At Dogs Trust rehoming centres, prospective owners are asked to fill in a questionnaire when they first arrive. The questions include the following:

- **What size of dog are you looking for?**
  Dogs vary in size from the tinies to the giants, with lots of different sizes in between. You need to consider whether you have the space to take on a bigger dog at home – and whether there is enough room in the car!

Try to be clear in your own mind about the type of dog you want.

- **What age of dog are you looking for?**
  Puppies do come up for rehoming – and they usually go like hot cakes. In most cases, it is adult dogs who need a fresh start, and these can vary from youngsters under two years of age right up to veterans, aged eight years and over. You may feel that a younger dog will be more ready to adapt to a new home, but think carefully before taking on a boisterous 'teenager'. If you prefer a slower pace of life, an older dog may be more suitable. There are dogs who need rehoming because their owners have died or are too frail to care for them. These dogs may not be in the first flush of youth, but they still have plenty to offer, and there may be fewer training issues involved.

It can be hard to find homes for older dogs, but Amos, a ten-year-old German Shepherd Dog, spent only two days at the Dogs Trust rehoming centre at Salisbury before Paul and Amanda Smith spotted him and decided he was the dog for them.

"We rehomed a Yorkshire Terrier from a couple who had a baby and didn't want him anymore," said Paul. "When he died, the house seemed very empty, My wife is seriously ill, and has to spend a lot of time in bed, and it was very lonely for me.

"We went to the rehoming centre at Salisbury with our son, and saw a German Shepherd behind the counter. I thought he belonged to one of the staff, but then we found out he was up for rehoming. He had a tennis ball, and he jumped up and asked my son to throw it for him. From that moment, we knew he was the dog for us.

"Unfortunately, we couldn't find out anything about Amos. He had been at Salisbury for just two days, and he was one of a number of dogs who had been sent over from the rehoming centre at Shoreham because they were having building work done. I honestly have no idea why anyone would want to give him up. He's well trained, and he has settled in with no problems.

"He loves all the family – we have a 14-year-old son and a 15-year-old daughter – but he has

Amos: An older dog who deserved a second chance.

attached himself to me. I think that's because I spend most time with him. I feed him, and I take him out for his walks.

"I have always admired German Shepherds – I have wanted one ever since I was little, and Amos has turned out to be all I hoped. He may be ten years old, but he's a big baby. He's mad about his tennis ball – he would play with it all day if you let him.

"He can be a bit funny with other dogs, so I take him out at times when we are unlikely to meet any. We want to overcome the problem, so we asked a professional trainer to assess him. He reckons that Amos gets over-excited with other dogs, and doesn't know how to react. We are now letting him off the lead, but giving him something to focus on, such as his tennis ball. If Amos can overcome his problem with other dogs, we would seriously think about rehoming another dog.

"I know some people think you are taking on problems if you rehome a dog. But if you go out and buy a puppy, you don't know how it's going to turn out. You know how you would like the dog to be, but there are no guarantees. If you rehome an older dog, you know exactly what you're getting. We got to know Amos, and so we knew he would be the sort of dog who would fit in with our family. It's also nice to think you are giving a dog a second chance – particularly a dog like Amos, who has never done anything wrong."

• **Do you want a male or a female?**
You may have strong feelings about the sex of your dog, or you may not consider it to be a big issue. All dogs that are rehomed from Dogs Trust are neutered, and this is true of many rehoming organisations. This means that you do not have to cope with a bitch's seasonal cycle, and a neutered male is less likely to stray from home looking for bitches in season.

However, you should bear in mind that male and female characteristics will still be in evidence even though a dog has been neutered. This is rarely a problem with bitches. Apart from ensuring that she does not gain too much weight (see page 58), you will enjoy the freedom of owning a bitch who no longer comes into season or suffers from false pregnancies.

Neutering is often seen as a way of calming a male dog and reducing dominant or aggressive behaviour (see page 110). This is true to a certain extent, but a lot depends on what age the dog is castrated. If a male is fully mature, and certain types of behaviour have become habitual, he will probably behave in much the same way after neutering. Ideally, a male should be neutered when he has reached sexual maturity (on average 9-10 months, depending on breed/size). In this way, he will be physically mature, but he will not have had the chance to develop the type of assertive behaviour that is often driven by hormones.

• **Do you live in a house, flat or bungalow?**
Again, this is relevant in terms of the size of dog you will be able to accommodate.

In some breeds and cross-breeds, the male may be a large and powerful animal.

• **Do you have a garden?**
It is possible to keep a dog if you do not have a garden, but it certainly makes life an awful lot harder. If you do not have a garden, you will have to provide a complete exercise programme, and you will also have to find a nearby toilet area, which you must keep scrupulously clean. In this situation, an older dog who does not need so much exercise may be a good choice.

• **Is your garden enclosed? What height is the fencing?**
It is essential to have a secure garden, which a dog cannot escape from. Some dogs have no thought of trying to leave their new home; others are canine Houdinis, who will always try to find a way out. The escape artist might try to leap the fence, dig his way out, or push through a gate that has a faulty fastening. You will need to check that your garden is secure, and that the fencing is of a suitable height. Generally, a minimum height of 5 ft (1.52 m) is recommended, but for bigger dogs with a history of escaping, the fencing should be 6 ft (1.82 m) tall.

• **Who lives at home?**
This is a vitally important question, as the make-up of your family will be a highly influential factor in deciding whether a dog is suitable for you. Some dogs love people of all ages, but if you have a baby, or toddlers, a big, bouncy dog may be too much to handle. Some dogs are better with children who are older, and some dogs don't like children at all. In most cases, the rehoming organisations will know the background of the dogs they are offering, and unless a dog is known to be trustworthy with children, it is better to rehome him somewhere where children are not present.

If you have small children, it may be worth waiting until a puppy comes up for rehoming. This may seem like harder work in the short term, but raising puppies and children together can work out better than trying to introduce an adult dog into a family situation.

- **Will your dog be left alone at home?**
  Most rehoming organisations stipulate that a dog should not be left on his own for more than four hours at a stretch. If you are taking on a puppy, this will be too long to begin with. You will need to gradually build up the amount of time the dog can be left (see page 107). It may be possible to come home in the middle of the day to exercise your dog and to spend some time with him, or to arrange for a dog-sitter, but you cannot consider owning a dog if everyone in the family is out all day.

- **Do you own other dogs?**
  Care must always be taken when introducing a new dog. In the case of a rescued dog, it is important to find out as much as possible about his background to see if he gets on with other dogs. The rehoming agency will also check out this aspect of behaviour. Expert staff at the centre may work on improving dog-to-dog relations, but there are some dogs who will never live in harmony with another dog, so they need to be the only dog in a family.

- **Do you own other pets?**
  Cats can be a source of trouble in some breeds and breed types. For example, Greyhounds and Lurchers have a strong instinct to chase, and may be unreliable with cats and other small animals. The rehoming organisation will have made efforts to check out this aspect of a dog's behaviour, and so it is important to follow their advice.

- **How much daily exercise can you give your dog?**
  Note that the question refers to daily exercise. If you have a young, lively dog, such as a Border Collie type, he will not be content

You will need to go for a dog who is known to be sociable if you already have a dog at home.

with a marathon walk at the weekend and nothing in-between. You need to work out how much exercise you can give your dog every day, and this can be matched to the requirements of the dogs on offer.

- **What is your experience with dogs?** If you have never owned a dog before, it does not rule you out for adopting a rescued dog. However, be aware that you are taking on a bigger challenge, and you must be prepared to seek help and advice with training. If you have owned dogs previously, be honest about how much training you have done and whether you relish the prospect of training a rescued dog who may have some behavioural problems to overcome. There is no sense in taking on a dog that is beyond your capabilities, as it will only end in disaster.

ASSESSING THE DOGS

In order to make good matches, the rehoming centre needs to build up a case history for every dog in its care. Where possible, this involves getting as much background information on the dog as possible. This is relatively easy if the owners gave up the dog for adoption, but in the

The rehoming agency will gather as much information as possible when a dog is put up for adoption.

case of strays, it may be impossible to find out anything at all. In this instance, the vet at the rehoming centre will examine the dog and give an opinion as to the age and breed type.

If the dog is full grown, staff can make a fairly good guess as to breed type. A vet can examine the condition of the teeth, which is a reasonably accurate method of ageing a dog.

HAND-OVER

If a dog is being relinquished by his owners and handed over to a rehoming centre, there is the opportunity to compile a detailed case history of the dog. Dogs Trust has compiled a form to be filled in by the owners who are giving up the dog. This includes some of the following questions:

GENERAL
- How long have you had the dog?
- Where did you obtain your dog?

HEALTH
- Is your dog neutered? If so, when?
- If female, when was she last in season?
- When did your dog last visit a vet, and for what reason?

- Does your dog have any special medical or nutritional requirements?

BEHAVIOUR

- Has your dog ever bitten, or shown signs of aggression?
- Does your dog have any fears or phobias, e.g. fireworks, thunder?

CONTACT

Has your dog had contact with:
- *Children?* Did he enjoy being with them, tolerate them, ignore them, or avoid them? Would you rehome this dog with children?
- *Cats?* Were there any problems? Would you place this dog in a home with cats?
- *Dogs?* Would you place your dog in a home with other dogs?
- *Livestock?* Were there any problems? Would you rehome this dog near livestock?

ENVIRONMENT

Is your household:
- Busy?
- Quiet?
- In-between?

AT HOME

- How long is your dog left alone on a normal weekday?
- How does your dog react when left alone? (Good? Clean? Destructive? Dirty? Sleeps? Barks? Plays with toys?)
- How does your dog react when left in the garden? (Good? Jumps fences? Digs? Barks?)
- How does your dog react to visitors? (Good? Growls? Excitable? Snaps? Ignores? Bites?)

GROOMING

When being groomed, does your dog:
- Fidget?
- Mouth the brush?
- Stand still?
- Growl?
- Enjoy being groomed?
- Refuse to be groomed?

TRAVELLING

- Is your dog used to travelling in the car?
- How does your dog react when travelling? (Barks? Quiet? Restless? Jumps around? Sick?)
- Is your dog okay to be left in the car?

TRAINING AND PLAYING

- Can you take toys away from your dog?
- Which is your dog's favourite game?
- Is your dog allowed off the lead?
- Does your dog return on command?
- Which of these commands does your dog know? (Sit? Down? Stay? Drop? Recall?)
- What does your dog enjoy the most? (Food? Toys? Being stroked? Walks? Chase games? People? Other animals? Bikes/cars?)

OTHER INFORMATION

- Is there anything else you think we should know about your dog?
- Why are you giving up the dog for adoption?

Once these questions have been answered, expert training and behaviour advisors at the rehoming centre can build up a very accurate picture of the dog. In addition, staff will carry out their own checks and add further comments to the dog's case history.

AT THE CENTRE

A dog who comes in for rehoming will undergo a thorough physical examination. The vet will assess a dog's overall condition as well as pinpointing any health problems. If there is no known history, the dog will start a course of vaccinations. Routine preventative health care, such as worming and flea protection, will also be administered. This is really like an MOT for dogs, and comments about the dog's health or behaviour when being handled will be added to his case notes.

The dog will then be handed over to the kennel staff, who will bath him and groom him. Teeth may be cleaned and nails will be trimmed (see pages 59-60). Again, comments on the dog's behaviour will be added to his file.

Ideally, dogs are kennelled in pairs, as this gives the benefit of company. Great care is taken when introducing two dogs, and they are closely supervised until staff are happy that the pair get on together. Obviously, a dog with a history of antisocial behaviour with other dogs will be kennelled separately.

Dogs that come in for rehoming are given a thorough grooming. This dog needed to have the hair trimmed around his feet.

TEMPERAMENT-TESTING

When a dog has been at the rehoming centre for about a week, he will be given a temperament assessment. The aim is to see if the dog's behaviour ties in with the information provided by his previous owners. If the dog has no case notes, the tester will need to evaluate the dog's temperament to the best of his or her ability.

Initially, the dog will be tested to see if he is happy to be handled.
• The dog will be stroked all over.
• Each paw will be picked up in turn.
• The dog's ears and eyes will be examined.
• The dog's teeth will be inspected.

As well as checking over the dog, this gives a good indication of whether a dog is co-operative when he is being handled, whether he is excitable, whether he is nervous, or whether he resists the attention by growling or backing off. Comments made by the vet, and also the kennel staff who have been looking after the dog, will also be taken into consideration.

BEHAVIOUR WITH OTHER DOGS

This is tested when preparing to kennel two dogs together. If a dog is known to be aggressive with other dogs, this will be assessed in a controlled situation to evaluate the extent of the problem. Dogs Trust has a behaviour and training advisor at most of its centres, and they will supervise these more problematic interactions.

REACTION TO CATS

In many cases, a rehoming centre will have a bomb-proof resident cat, who doesn't turn a hair when confronted by excitable dogs. The

At Dogs Trust interaction between dogs is carefully supervised, and their behaviour is noted.

dog will be put on a lead, and, as he is walked past the cat, his reaction will be noted. If the dog does not take too much notice of the cat, or is easily distracted from looking at it, he would be considered okay with cats. Extreme interest or attempts to lunge at the cat would rule out a home with a pet cat.

LEFT ALONE

It is important to find out if a dog will tolerate being left on his own. Again, information may be provided by the previous owners, but the behaviour will also be tested at the centre. At Dogs Trust rehoming centres, there are 'real life' rooms where a dog can be left on his own. The room will have the type of furniture that is found in the average sitting room – armchairs, a table and a television. The dog will be left for a

period of time and his behaviour will be noted. There are some dogs who suffer from separation anxiety, and they become very distressed when they are left on their own. This type of dog can be helped to overcome his problems (see pages 106-107), but potential owners need to be aware of the behaviour.

A FULL PICTURE

By the time a dog has settled in kennels and gone through his assessment, staff will have a good idea of the behaviour and trainability of the dog that is to be rehomed. The information is kept on file, and added to where appropriate. When a prospective owner takes an interest in a particular dog, all the details will be available, and rehoming staff can help the prospective owner to decide whether the dog is suitable.

It is in everyone's interest if a dog can be rehomed as quickly as possible.

LIVING IN KENNELS

A kennel environment is very stressful for a dog who is used to living in a family. There is the constant noise of dogs barking and whining, and although kennel staff work hard at getting to know the dogs in their care, interaction with people is inevitably limited. At Dogs Trust rehoming centres, the dogs are allowed access to a paddock every day and they are also given a daily walk. However, there are many hours in the day, and a kennelled dog can easily become bored and frustrated.

Like people, dogs respond to stress in different ways. There are some laid-back types who seem to take everything in their stride, but most dogs find kennel life to be a challenge. A dog may become an incessant barker, or spend his time running up and down the run, or even bouncing off the walls. Another type of dog may become withdrawn or nervous. When you consider that these dogs have already become unsettled by leaving their home and family, it is hardly surprising that they become upset. It is therefore in everyone's interests that a dog is rehomed as quickly as possible.

MAKING THE CHOICE

When you have gone round the kennels and looked at all the dogs that are available, you need to make a shortlist of the dogs that most appeal to you. Staff at the rehoming centre will then fill you in on the case history of each dog, and you can see if there is a suitable match.

If there is a dog that you like, and who appears to be right for your lifestyle and family circumstances, the next step is to get to know the dog better. Dogs Trust recommends two or three visits, bringing along all members of the family. There will be an opportunity to walk the dog on a lead, and to go into one of the 'real life' rooms so the prospective owners can see how the dog reacts in a confined space. This is particularly useful if there is a family with small children. The dog may seem easy to handle when he is on-lead in an open space, but it can be quite a different story when everyone is at close quarters.

If the family already has a dog, initial introductions are made at the rehoming centre to see how the two dogs react. Obviously, rehoming staff will have checked that the rescued dog gets on with other dogs before matching him, but expert help is needed to get the relationship off to a sound start.

At Dogs Trust, the drill adopted is to take the dogs to an open space, such as a field, and to lead-walk the two dogs side by side, with a reasonable space in-between. Head-on meetings should be avoided in the initial stages. Observing the body language of the two dogs is the key to reading their reactions, and so a training and behaviour expert will usually supervise the introduction. If the dogs are happy – taking an interest in each other, but showing no overt aggression – the space between them can be closed up so that the two dogs are walking next to each other. If everything is going well, the dogs will be allowed off-lead. Generally, by this stage, the dogs will be ready to interact with each other. If any negative signs have been picked up, further consideration will be given as to whether the rescued dog should be placed in a home that already has a dog.

HOME VISIT

Most rehoming organisations plan a home visit before a rescued dog is formally adopted. This is to check that the home is suitable for the type of dog that has been selected, and to check that the garden is secure and the fencing is the required height.

REFERENCES

Many rehoming charities will take up references before the adoption goes through. If you already have a dog, or have had one in the recent past, Dogs Trust asks for a reference from your vet. If you have not owned a dog before, you may be asked to find a vet in your area who will be able to give help and advice when your dog first arrives home.

PRE-ADOPTION TALK

At Dogs Trust rehoming centres, prospective owners are asked to attend a talk before the adoption goes through. This is to give general advice about caring for a dog, and also to give guidance on training issues. Obviously, the dogs that are to be rehomed will all be different, but taking on a rescued dog presents particular challenges, and it is important that owners are fully aware of all that is involved before making the final commitment.

PAPERWORK

When all parties are happy that the correct match has been made, it is time for the new owners to formally adopt their dog. In most cases, a small donation is required to cover some of the costs of microchipping and neutering. The owners are then ready to take full responsibility for the dog.

At Dogs Trust, and many of the other rehoming charities, post-adoption support is provided if necessary. This may take the form of training classes held at the rehoming centre, access to a telephone advice helpline, or it may even involve a home visit to help sort out training difficulties. The aim is to rehome a dog for life, and so help is always available in the early stages when a dog is settling into his new home.

CHAPTER THREE

GETTING READY

While you are waiting for the adoption to go through, you can spend your time getting ready for the new arrival. Dogs do not require a great deal in the way of equipment, but there are a few essentials that you should buy in advance.

BEDS & BEDDING

Every dog needs his own place to sleep. He should see his bed as his private quarters – where he feels safe and secure, and is allowed to rest in peace.

There are a wide variety of dog beds on the market, ranging from cosy cushions to wicker baskets. The type of bed you choose will obviously depend on the size of dog. One of the most practical options is a plastic kidney-shaped bed, which you can line with bedding. These are virtually indestructible and are easy to clean. They come in lots of different sizes, which can accommodate anything from a Chihuahua to a Great Dane.

The best bedding to buy is synthetic fleece.

Buy two pieces – one to use and one as a spare. This type of bedding is comfortable for the dog; it is machine-washable and dries quickly.

All dogs like their creature comforts, but none more so than Greyhounds and Lurchers. These dogs really crave a cosy bed, and many owners have found that buying a cheap duvet and a couple of covers is an ideal solution.

Your dog will need a cosy bed to sleep in.

CAR TRAVEL

It is advisable for a dog to be confined in one area of the car. The dog will soon learn that this is his place, and he will learn to settle. A dog who is allowed to jump from seat to seat will get wildly over-excited, and could prove a real danger to the driver.

If you are adopting a small dog, you could invest in a carrier, which can be placed on the back seat (secured with a strap). The carrier will also come in useful for vet visits.

A bigger dog will be better off in the rear of the car. A dog guard will confine the dog to his area, and if you put down some bedding, he will

Decide which areas of the house your dog is allowed in before he arrives home.

soon learn to settle. The other option is to buy a travel harness, which is fitted to the dog, and is secured using a seatbelt. The great advantage of this is that if you are involved in an accident, the dog is less likely to be injured – and is less likely to injure you.

For more information on car travel, see page 98.

STAIR-GATE

This may seem a strange purchase for a dog, but it can come in very handy. For example, you may not want your dog to go upstairs until he learns the house rules (see page 75). If your dog is anxious and needs to learn to spend time alone, a stair-gate is an invaluable training aid (see page 107).

COLLAR/LEAD

Your dog will need a collar and lead. Again, seek advice from the rehoming centre staff so that you buy the right size. Greyhounds and Lurchers will need a special fish-shaped collar (wide in the middle), which is designed especially for the breed. These are available from pet stores.

The lead should suit the size and strength of your dog, and should have a secure trigger fastening. It is better to avoid chain leads, as these can be harsh on the hands, particularly if you have a dog who tends to pull.

It is a good idea to buy a flexible, extending lead. It is generally recommended that a rescued dog should not be let off the lead for six weeks after arriving in his new home, so the flexible lead will be very useful during this period. Practise using it in the garden before venturing into the outside world so that you can operate it with confidence.

However, a flexible lead should not be used when you are walking on the road, just in case your dog suddenly pulls and you lose control of the lead. If you have to walk to your park or local exercise area, use an ordinary lead, and then swap to the extended lead when you arrive.

At the rehoming centre, you will have had the chance to walk your dog on a lead. You will know from this whether your dog tends to pull. If you foresee this being a problem, you may want to look at the anti-pull devices that have been designed specifically to help overcome this problem. You can try a half-check collar, which is safe to use because it does not close fully on the neck when the dog pulls.

If your dog does not respond to the half-check collar, try a head collar, which puts pressure on the muzzle rather than around the neck. There are a variety of designs, which include the Halti, The Gentle Leader, and the Dogalter. It is best to seek the advice of the training expert at the rehoming centre if you know your dog pulls on the lead.

For advice on lead-training, see pages 79-82.

ID

In many cases, your dog will be microchipped by the rehoming organisation prior to adoption. But he will still need a form of ID on his collar. Most pet stores can provide engraved discs. Essential details include your name (the dog's name is optional), and your address and phone number.

FEEDING BOWLS

Your dog will need two feeding bowls: one for food and one for water. Plastic bowls are bright and colourful, but they are easily chewed. Stainless steel bowls, which last forever and are easy to clean, may be a better option. Some owners like to use an earthenware bowl for drinking water. This type of bowl is fine, but it is breakable.

FOOD

Find out what your dog is being fed at the rehoming centre, and then get a supply. If a dog changes diet suddenly, it is likely to lead to stomach upsets, so it is better to stick to the food he is used to, at least to begin with.

For more information on feeding, see pages 57-58.

At Dogs Trust, all dogs are microchipped before going to their new homes.

OUTDOOR DOG COAT

This is very much a fashion garment, and there is no need to buy one unless you want to. The exception is if you are adopting a Whippet or a Greyhound. These breeds have a fine coat, and they really do feel the cold.

GROOMING GEAR

The type of brushes and combs you buy will depend on your dog's coat type. Many rehoming centres have a specialist groomer, and you can ask advice as to what your dog needs. Remember that grooming is an important part of caring for your dog, and even if the dog you are planning to adopt is a short-coated, low-maintenance type, he will still need to be brushed and combed on a regular basis. Grooming is also a good way of developing a relationship with your dog.

For more information on grooming, see page 60.

DENTAL CARE

You will need to buy a toothbrush and toothpaste for your dog. You can use a finger brush or a long-handled toothbrush, depending on which you find easier. There are lots of doggie toothpastes on the market in a variety of meaty flavours (see page 60).

NAIL-CLIPPERS

You may need to trim your dog's nails if they do not wear down naturally. This is always the case with Greyhounds, who have long nails, but most types of dog need a nail trim from time to time. The best nail-clippers to buy are the guillotine type. The other option is to buy a nail file, which does the job just as effectively, but it does take time (see page 59).

TOYS

These are fun to buy, and there is no shortage of choice. In fact, toys can be dual purpose, as you can use them as a training aid (see page 72) as well as letting your dog play with them.

It is essential to check that the toys you buy are 100 per cent safe. A dog can chew through plastic in no time, and this is potentially hazardous if the dog swallows large chunks of plastic, or gets hold of the squeaker in a toy. The safest toys to buy are those that are made of hard rubber, or cotton tug toys.

WARNING

If you are planning to adopt one of the guarding breeds, such as a German Shepherd or a Rottweiler, or a dog that is closely related to these breeds, avoid buying tug-of-war toys. Although it may appear like harmless fun to have a game of tug with your dog, it can help to stimulate instincts to run and bite, which is the last thing you want.

BOREDOM BUSTERS

There are now a number of toys specially designed to keep a dog occupied. The toy has hiding places to secrete food, and the dog not only has to find out where the food is, he has to work hard to get it! These are excellent toys to use when your dog has to be left on his own for a period of time (see page 107).

CLEAN UP!

If your dog fouls in a public place, you will need to clean up after him. You can buy a pooper scooper and/or plastic bags for this – never leave home without them!

Make sure that the toys you buy are 100 per cent safe.

PREPARING YOUR HOME

If the rehoming centre requests a home visit, you will be given advice on adapting your house and garden so that they are suitable for a dog.

The most important consideration is deciding where your dog is going to sleep. He will need somewhere that is warm and cosy in the winter, relatively cool in the summer, and free from draughts. Many people find that the kitchen or utility room is the best place to locate the dog bed or crate.

If you want your dog to have his own special place in the sitting room (even though he sleeps in the utility room), you can always buy a second bed, or just use some bedding so that your dog has his own spot.

As far as the rest of the house is concerned, the byword is better safe than sorry. If you are adopting a puppy, you know that the pup is likely to chew, and so it is sensible to keep

valuables out of his reach. An adult dog is less likely to chew, but if he is anxious and worried as he settles into his new home, he may regress to puppy-like behaviour. If you are rehoming a Greyhound who has spent his life in kennels, or a stray who has lived on the streets, the dog will not be used to a home environment.

Obviously you want to get relations off to a good start, rather than having to reprimand the dog as soon as he steps over the threshold, so take the following precautions:

- Secure trailing electric cables so that they are out of your dog's reach.
- Relocate potted plants (which may be poisonous) and any other ornamental displays (e.g. dried flower arrangements) so the dog cannot get at them – and that includes when he is jumping up and wagging his tail.
- Check the fastening of food cupboards if they

Fencing must be the appropriate height for the size of dog you are planning to adopt.

are located at ground level. This applies particularly to the cupboard where you store your dog's food. Obviously, the food is a source of temptation, but if a dog breaks into a cupboard and gorges on a dry, complete diet, the results could be fatal.

- Ensure that household cleaners, such as bleach and disinfectant, are kept in a secure cupboard.
- An overhanging tablecloth may be worthy of a tug – so it may be better to dispense with it rather than seeing your dinner going flying!
- Get in the habit of tidying up. If you leave your slippers lying about, you cannot entirely blame your dog for getting hold of them.
- If you have children, encourage them to keep their toys in a safe place, which the dog cannot reach. There are many incidents of children being upset because toys are ruined –

and just as many instances of a dog being rushed to the vet because he has swallowed part of a toy.

IN THE GARDEN

The garden will be checked when you have your home visit to see that the fencing is secure and is the appropriate height for the dog you are planning to adopt (see page 31). It is also important to check that gate fastenings are secure, and to encourage all members of the family to get into the habit of keeping the gate closed.

You will also need to check out the following:

- If you have a garden shed where you keep pesticides, it must be 100 per cent secure.
- If you have a garden pond, it is worth considering some form of covering. Some

dogs cannot resist taking a dip, and an enthusiastic swimmer, such as a Labrador, can ruin an ornamental pond in seconds!

- Make sure rubbish bins are located in an area that your dog cannot get at, or find some means of securing the lids (luggage straps are ideal). Your dog may take no notice of the bins, but if he is used to scavenging, it will be a ready source of temptation.
- Check the plants in your garden – there are a number that are poisonous to dogs. For a full listing of plants that are poisonous to dogs, visit the Dogs Trust website at: www.dogstrust.org.uk

NAME CHANGE

Choosing a name is a fun aspect of owning a pet, but if you take on a rescued dog, you should give the matter careful consideration.

Your dog may have arrived at the rehoming centre with no name. The staff will have given him a temporary name, but there is no need to stick with it. The dog is unlikely to have made a close connection with it, and you will probably want a new name to go with the dog's new start.

If a dog comes into the rehoming centre with a known name, you should think twice before changing it. As far as the dog is concerned, a new name is just one more change in a life that is full of uncertainties. A bright dog will soon catch on to his new name, but it may make it easier if you choose a name that sounds similar. For example, Lottie could be changed to Lettie, and the dog will scarcely notice the switch.

An inquisitive dog will explore every nook and cranny.

POISONOUS PLANTS CHECKLIST

• Amarylis	• Milkweed
• Azalea	• Mistletoe
• Cyclamen	• Nightshade
• Daffodil bulbs	• Oleander
• Dumb cane (dieffenbachia)	• Philodendron
• Elderberry	• Poinsettia
• English ivy	• Primrose
• Foxglove	• Privet
• Holly berries	• Ragwort
• Hyacinth	• Rhododendron
• Iris	• Spider plant
• Laurel	• Stinging nettle
• Lily of the valley	• Wisteria
	• Yew

Carol Shreeve and her partner, Andy, thought long and hard before deciding to adopt a dog. A litter of mixed-breed pups was put up for rehoming at the Dogs Trust centre in Darlington. That was when Millie came into their lives – and then, two weeks later, her litter sister, Mia, came to join the family home. Life has never been the same since…

"The puppies' mother was a stray, and she was found when she was heavily pregnant," said Carol. "A small charity took her in when she had the pups, and then they were handed over to Dogs Trust.

"Initially, we thought about adopting an older dog, but when these pups came up, we decided to go for one. We have a cat, Orwell, who is now 15, and we decided it would be easier for her to accept a puppy rather than an older dog.

"Millie had been with us for two weeks when we heard that things had not worked out for one of the other bitches in the litter, and she needed a home. That was when we agreed to take on Mia.

"We knew we were taking on a big commitment with one pup, and realised that this was going to have a big impact on our lives. Dogs Trust was amazingly helpful, and gave us lots of information about dog care and training. We also know lots of people who have dogs, so we had support.

"In fact, it has worked out better for us having two dogs at the same time. We both work from home, and I think we could have had problems with over-bonding if there was only one dog. The two dogs play with each other and enjoy each other's company.

LEARNING TOGETHER

"They can be a bit of a handful, particularly when they get over-excited, but our friends are dog-friendly and know the right way to behave. In terms of training, we have sometimes separated the two dogs, but mostly they seem to learn from each other. It is important to treat them as individuals and to appreciate that they learn at a different pace from each other.

"We have no idea of their breeding. There may be a bit of Greyhound in there somewhere, but I think there is so much mixed blood, you can't work out specific breeds. They are both black and tan, but Mia is quite a bit smaller than Millie. Mia has a short coat, whereas Millie has a short coat with feathering.

DIFFERENT TYPES

"They have completely different personalities. Millie is daft dog with big, floppy ears. She loves dogs and people, and she's a great enthusiast. Mia is also very loving, but she's very smart. She has already learned to open doors with handles, and so we have to fit locking devices on the cupboards.

"When you first meet her, Mia seems the better behaved of the two, but you always have the feeling she's plotting something. She's certainly the more dominant of the two, and she is quick to put Millie in her place.

"Orwell, the cat, has not been too much put out by the puppies. We have a stair-gate so the pups cannot go upstairs, and that gives her personal space, which is very important. She comes downstairs a lot, but if the dogs get too boisterous, she can escape. In fact, the dogs look on the cat as their pack leader, rather than either of us. If one of them steps out of line, Orwell gives a quick swipe with her paw, and the dogs respect her.

"Before we had the dogs, we did not have much in the way of commitments, and we could please ourselves. Now everything has changed. We have to get up to let the dogs out, we have to feed them and exercise them – but the benefits far outweigh the drawbacks. We have so much fun with the dogs. They give us a sense of responsibility, and they make our house into a family home."

Millie (left) and Mia: The two pups seem to learn from each other.

CHAPTER FOUR

SETTLING IN

At last, all the paperwork has been completed and it is time to collect your dog. This is a hugely exciting moment, and it is tempting to pack the car with friends and family. But first think how traumatic this move will be for your new pet.

If you are adopting a puppy, this may be the first time he has been separated from his littermates, so he is bound to feel bewildered. If you are taking on an older dog, the experience will be even more stressful. The dog may have been in kennels for a short time, and just as he was beginning to settle, he is being taken away by people he doesn't know. Alternatively, you may be adopting a long-stay resident who has come to look on the rehoming centre as his home.

All you want to do is to reassure your dog, and tell him that this is the start of a bright, new future. However, this is a case where actions definitely speak louder than words. Do everything you can to make the move as easy as possible.

- Go to the rehoming centre with one other adult, who can drive the car while you look after the dog.
- If you are adopting a puppy, your 'helper' can drive while you hold the pup in your lap.
- An adult dog will need to be confined safely in the car, so you will need to have made suitable preparations (see page 34).
- Go equipped with some paper towelling in case of accidents, or if your dog is car sick.
- If it is a hot day, and you have a long journey, take a bottle of drinking water and a bowl.
- Arrange to collect your dog in the morning so he has the maximum amount of time to settle in his new home before nightfall.
- Try not to stop on your journey home. If you have a long way to travel and need to take a break, make sure the dog has his collar securely fastened and his lead attached before you let him out of the car. Remember that this is a very confusing time for your new dog, and you do not want to risk him taking off in fright.

At last, the big day arrives when it is time to collect your dog.

ARRIVING HOME

When you arrive home, take your dog into the garden. He will need a chance to relieve himself after the journey, and he can explore his new surroundings off-lead. If you have a puppy, you will need to start a housetraining programme straightaway. If you have an adult, he may be reliable in his housetraining, or he may need to learn what is required (see page 52). In all cases, praise your dog enthusiastically when he performs, leaving him in no doubt that you are pleased with him.

Next, take your dog into the house, and show him his sleeping quarters. Let him sniff around and get used to the new environment. If you have an indoor kennel, you could put a treat inside so that the dog goes to investigate.

An adult dog who has been brought up in a home will soon find his feet. A puppy is obviously experiencing everything for the first time, but most pups will respond to

encouragement and reassurance. In fact, a bold pup will soon be into everything!

If you are adopting a dog who is not used to a home, you may find that he is more cautious, and, in some cases, he may be overwhelmed by his new situation. This applies particularly to ex-racing Greyhounds, who are only familiar with a kennel environment. For this type of dog, the sight of a television or the noise of a washing machine could be alarming.

If your dog appears nervous, let him explore at his own pace. Give him lots of praise when he starts to show some confidence, and do not push him further than he wants to go. It may be better if you let the dog get used to one room, and let him settle quietly in the kitchen, for example, before letting him look round the rest of the house.

A very nervous dog may, initially, be too frightened to be in the same room with you. In this situation, give the dog time and space to make up his own mind. If you overwhelm the dog with too much attention, he will feel threatened. The best plan is to keep the door open, and put a cosy blanket or duvet near the door. Most dogs (and all Greyhounds) cannot resist a cosy place to lie, and if you ignore the dog, he will eventually creep into the room and lie down on the bed. Gradually move the bed away from the door and into the main part of the room, and the dog will follow!

MEETING THE FAMILY

Hopefully, your dog will have met all members of his new family during the adoption process. But he now needs to meet everyone in his new home environment. It is important to take time with these interactions.

Some dogs will be excitable in this situation, so try to keep the atmosphere calm and relaxed. Let each person stroke the dog in turn, and perhaps give him a treat. Allow the dog to sniff each person so that he gets to know everyone's scent, and let him get used to the different voices in the family.

Resist the temptation to invite your friends and neighbours to come and meet the new arrival. It is important that your dog settles with his new family before he is exposed to more strangers.

CHILDREN

Staff at the rehoming centre will make every effort to help you choose a dog that is trustworthy with children. Ideally, you will be adopting a puppy, or a dog who is used to living with children. It is very hard for an older dog to adapt to a house full of children if he has not been used to them since puppyhood.

When your dog arrives home, you will need to supervise introductions with children.

- If you have a puppy, start by getting the children to sit on the floor, and let each child hold the pup in turn and give him a treat. Remember, pups do wriggle, and it is all too easy for them to be dropped, so interactions between puppies and children should be conducted at ground level.
- You can then let the pup run between the children. If each child has a treat, they can call the pup in turn, and reward him with a treat – his first recall lesson!
- If you have an adult dog, make sure the children are sitting on chairs or on the sofa when they are first introduced. An adult dog may become over-excited if children are at his level.

Children and dogs can be the best of friends, but it is essential to establish a sense of mutual respect.

A pup must learn to take treats or a toy gently.

- Again, let each child stroke the dog and give him a treat. Encourage the children to be as calm as possible – ban shouting and screaming!

PLAY SESSIONS

Always supervise interactions between your dog and young children. Games can get out of hand, and this could lead to trouble, particularly if you have a young, boisterous dog. Teach your children to be calm around the dog, and to keep the games low-key. A dog will get hyped up if he sees children running, or if he hears raised voices, and he will swiftly forget his manners.

FUN AND GAMES

- Children can play a version of the puppy recall game (see page 45), standing a distance apart, and then calling the dog to them in turn. Make sure the children have treats to reward the dog.
- You can graduate to a game of hide-and-seek outdoors. One child hides behind a tree or a bush, while the other child distracts the dog's attention. The child who is hiding calls the dog, and he has to seek him/her out. The child has a treat ready to reward the dog.
- If your dog enjoys retrieving, the children can play 'fetch' games with him. Make sure the dog gives up his toy on request, and prevent any attempts to tug the toy out of his mouth.

MOUTHING

Puppies in a litter are used to grabbing hold of each other, and mouthing is an extension of this. The puppy, or young dog, needs to learn that this is not acceptable behaviour with people.

To begin with, you must carry out the corrective training, but as soon as your dog understands what you are getting at, the children can join in.

- Offer your dog a treat, and as he goes to take it, say "Gently".
- If the dog tries to grab the treat, close your fist and do not let him have it.
- Offer the treat a second time, repeating the command "Gently". After a few tries, your dog will realise that he is only rewarded with his treat when he does not grab.
- You can make the situation more realistic by giving a sharp yelp if your dog tries to grab

you. In a litter, the pups yelp in protest when a game gets too rough, so your dog will understand the meaning.

- The next step is to try taking a toy from your dog. If your dog is the type that likes to hang on, make sure you have a treat or another toy at the ready, and then you can do a swap. As far as the dog is concerned, he has not lost his toy – he has gained a reward! Use the command "Give", and praise the dog the moment he co-operates.

It may take a little time for your dog to learn that he must inhibit his natural desire to mouth when he is interacting with people. But if you work at the exercises outlined above, he will gradually realise that his antisocial behaviour gets him nowhere, but when he does as you ask, he gets a reward.

GOLDEN RULES

Children and dogs can form close relationships, but it is very important that they both learn to respect each other. Stick to the following rules, and your dog will soon fit in with the bustle of family life.

FOR THE CHILDREN

- Never allow children to play with a dog unless they are supervised.
- Never allow children to tease a dog with toys or treats.
- Never allow children to be rough with the dog – pulling his ears or his tail, or poking him in the eye.
- Never allow children to disturb a dog when he is eating or sleeping.

FOR THE DOG

- The dog must never be allowed to mouth children.
- The dog must never be allowed to jump up, or chase children.
- The dog must never be allowed to beg for food.

NOTE: Dogs and children both love toys – and that can be a source of trouble. Children will be upset if the dog ruins a toy, and the dog may injure himself by swallowing part of a toy. Keep the dog away when children are playing with toys at ground level, and ensure that they tidy up after they have finished playing.

Keep your dog's toys where the children can reach them, and teach them to let the dog have one of his own toys if he tries to take one belonging to them.

Remember to make a fuss of the adult so he does not feel left out.

Simon and Simone Round, and their four children – Megan (13), Tom (11), Michael (22 months), and Mollie (9 months) – were used to having a dog in the family, so when their Lurcher, Boris, died at the grand old age of 14, they had no hesitation about getting another dog.

"It just seemed like the natural thing to do," said Simon. "Boris was so calm and gentle with the children that we decided to go for another sighthound breed. Simone was very keen to get a Greyhound, so we went to the Dogs Trust rehoming centre to see what they had.

"We were introduced to Ronnie, a big Greyhound who is a beautiful fawn colour. He has the most lovely face. We had all the children with us, and Ronnie did not seem at all fazed by them. We took him for a walk, and he walked along calmly on his lead. We were certain right from the start that he would fit in with the family.

SETTLING IN

"Ronnie is an ex-racing Greyhound, and he was tested unsafe with cats. That was okay, as we have no other pets. But apart from that, we had had no problems to cope with. Apparently, Ronnie had been allowed in his trainer's house, and so he was used to a home environment.

"The trainer also had young children, so Ronnie was used to children and was fine about settling in with the family. Our two older children know how to behave around dogs, but the little ones can be a bit more unpredictable. Michael likes to lean on Ronnie, but if it gets too much, Ronnie just gives a low grumble and moves away – there's nothing mean or aggressive about him.

CREATURE COMFORTS

"Ronnie's main objection was to our wooden floors, which he thought were a bit too hard for him. He decided the sofa was a much better idea. Now we have trained him to go in his dog bed, and he is quite happy to settle there.

"He really does love his food, and he would raid a bin or steal off the counter, given the chance. But he knows he must leave us alone at mealtimes. He lies in his bed and waits for us to finish.

"Like a lot of ex-racing Greyhounds, he is very good on the lead. He walks alongside the double pushchair, and you never have to give him a moment's thought.

PART OF THE FAMILY

"We have only had Ronnie for just over six months, but he is already very much part of the family. Our proudest moment was when we went to a country fair, and Megan, our eldest daughter, competed with him in an Obedience class. Much to our amazement, they came first – and a Greyhound coming first in Obedience is certainly something to celebrate!"

THE RESIDENT DOG

If you are adopting a puppy, the introduction is relatively straightforward. It is better if the meeting takes place in the garden, which is more like neutral territory. Put the adult dog on a lead, and let him sniff the new puppy. The pup should be on the ground rather than being held, so the adult dog does not feel as if you are confronting him with the new arrival.

- When the adult shows signs of being friendly, give him lots of praise and make a fuss of him.
- The pup will probably be submissive (ears back, and licking at the adult's mouth, or he may even roll over on to his back). Again, praise the adult if he stays calm and friendly.
- Now let the adult off-lead, and allow the two dogs to meet on their own terms. A bold pup will probably jump up at the adult and try to start a game. The adult may give a warning growl, but this is nothing to be alarmed about. The pup will have been disciplined by his mother, and he will understand that he must show a little more respect.
- Let the dogs get used to each other before going into the house. It does not take long for a pup and an adult to sort out their relationship, and you should have no further cause for concern.
- Do not let the two dogs sleep together overnight until you are confident that they are getting on well.
- With all the excitement of having a new puppy, it is easy for the resident dog to feel left out. Make sure you spend some quality time with the older dog, so that he knows he is a valued member of the family.

INTRODUCING AN OLDER DOG

If you are adopting an older dog, you will need to take more care with the introduction. A pup will instinctively submit to an older animal, whereas two adults are meeting on an equal footing, and they have to work out their relationship.

Hopefully, the two dogs will have had a chance to meet at the rehoming centre, but when you bring a new dog into the house, it is going to be more threatening for the resident dog.

- Start by letting the two dogs meet on neutral territory. You could take them both to the local park if it is within walking distance. However, you will need to ensure that two adults are present, so both dogs are fully under control.
- When you get to the park, keep both dogs on the lead, but make sure you do not put any tension on the lead.
- Walk the dogs next to each other (as you did at the rehoming centre), and if the dogs

Allow the dogs to meet on neutral territory, so the resident dog does not feel threatened.

appear unconcerned, let them stop and meet. Again, keep the leads as loose as possible, so that each dog is making his own decisions and not relying on you for back-up.

- It may be that one dog takes a more submissive role (tail down and ears back), while the other appears more confident (standing tall, with his tail waving like a flag). This is fine – the two dogs are communicating in their own language.

- If you are happy with the situation, let them off-lead. The dogs need to get to know each other and sort out their own relationship, so try not to interfere. If you get involved, it will confuse the situation, and the dogs will take much longer to resolve any differences they may have.

- When you get home, take both dogs into the garden. They will have more room, and the resident dog will not feel that his territory is being invaded in quite the same way as if the new dog came straight into the house.

The rehoming agency will have checked out a dog's reaction to cats before rehoming.

- Allow the dogs off-lead, and give the new dog a chance to explore. By this stage, they will be getting used to each other, and you can allow them to interact freely.

- Take the two dogs in the house, and, to begin with, do not pay too much attention to the new arrival. Let the dogs get used to being together without being fussed over, and they will quickly learn to live alongside each other in harmony.

- For the first few days, be on the safe side and do not leave the two dogs alone together.

MEETING THE CAT

If you have a cat at home, every effort will be made by the rescue organisation to ensure that the dog you adopt is feline-friendly. Many rehoming centres have a resident cat and so dogs can be tested to see how they react in a controlled situation (see pages 25 and 28).

However, it is important to bear in mind that even though your dog has been tested with a cat, it will be a different situation when you get him home. A newly adopted dog is bound to be tense and excitable, and your cat will certainly be alarmed by the presence of a strange dog in the house. What can you do to get relations off on the right footing?

PREPARATIONS

- Make sure the cat has places she can go where the dog is not allowed. For example, you can use a stair-gate, so that your dog cannot go upstairs but the cat can.

- Make sure the dog's sleeping quarters are not located in a place the cat regularly uses – such as en route to her cat flap.

- Place the cat's litter tray where it is inaccessible to your dog, and give the cat a chance to learn where you have put it. Some dogs cannot resist cat poo, and so it is best to prevent this antisocial behaviour becoming a habit.
- You can ask the rehoming centre to let you have a blanket that your dog has been lying on, so that the cat gets used to the scent of the dog before he arrives home.

PUPPY POWER

If you are adopting a puppy, introductions are relatively straightforward. The cat will not feel daunted by a small puppy in the same way she would with a larger, adult dog.

- If you have an indoor kennel, you can confine the pup and give the cat a chance to go up and investigate. If not, hold the pup in your lap, making sure he does not wriggle free!
- Distract the pup's attention with a treat, and when he focuses on you rather than the cat, praise him.
- You can then progress to letting the pup go free. Make sure the door is closed so the cat cannot run away, but also ensure she has a higher place to escape to, so that she feels safe. Again, distract the pup's attention from the cat, and reward him.
- Supervise all interactions for the first few days until the pair get used to each other.

THE OLDER DOG

The trigger that stimulates a dog to chase a cat is seeing her run. Your objective must be to avoid this situation from arising.

In time, a dog and a cat will learn to live in harmony.

- Put your dog on the lead, and allow him to look at the cat. Make sure the cat has a higher place she can escape to, if she feels threatened.
- Call the dog, and give him a treat when he looks away from the cat. Repeat this several times, each time rewarding the dog when he stops focusing on her.
- If your dog appears excitable, you may want to work at this controlled introduction over a few days. However, you will need to be 100 per cent sure that you avoid chance meetings during this period.
- If the cat settles, stay in the room for a while, with your dog sitting or lying beside you.

Hold the dog on a loose lead to avoid any sudden movements. The novelty for both animals will wear off if they spend some time together in a controlled situation.

• If the cat and dog appear reasonably calm and relaxed, you can progress to letting your dog off the lead. Make sure you have plenty of treats so that you can distract the dog if he shows too much interest in his feline friend.

If you supervise all interactions between your cat and your dog for the first few weeks, you will find that the two animals will learn to live in harmony. Remember that your dog may forget his good manners if he comes across the cat in the garden, so check that the cat is in the house before letting your dog out.

SIGHTHOUNDS AND CATS

Greyhounds and Lurchers are bred to chase, and they are rarely to be trusted with cats and other small animals, particularly if the dog has been racing. The rehoming centre will carry out a cat test and, in most cases, the dog will go to a home without a cat.

However, there are always exceptions to the rule, and there are stories of wonderful relationships developing between cats and Greyhounds. This is more often the case if the resident cat is used to dogs and stands her ground.

The best advice is never to take anything for granted – even if you have been told that your Greyhound or Lurcher is safe with cats. Err on the side caution and carry out initial introductions between cat and dog with the dog wearing a muzzle.

SMALL PETS

If you keep small animals, such as rabbits or guinea pigs, or you have a bird in a cage, your dog will need to learn that these fascinating creatures are members of his new family and must be respected.

• Put your dog on-lead (if you have a pup, you can hold him), and take him up to the cage/hutch.
• Let the dog look and sniff, and then distract him by calling his name. As soon as he responds, give him a treat.
• If your dog is focused on the animal, tell him "No" or "Leave" in a firm voice. As soon as he pays attention to you, reward him with a treat.
• You may find that your dog responds to a toy, and when you call him, you can throw his toy. The aim is to reward the dog when he focuses on you rather than the cage/hutch.
• Repeat this exercise over a number of days, before allowing your dog off-lead. In time, he will lose interest in the cage/hutch and will ignore it. However, do not allow your dog to be unsupervised in this situation – it is too great a risk to take, even if your dog appears to be trustworthy.

HOUSETRAINING

The dog you adopt may be perfectly housetrained. This is most likely to be the case if he has had a short stay in the rehoming centre, and was well cared for in his original home. However, there are other scenarios that may be applicable:

Housetraining should start from the moment a puppy arrives in his new home.

- If you have adopted a puppy, you will need to start housetraining from scratch.
- You may have taken on an ex-racing Greyhound who has only lived in kennels, or you may have adopted a long-stay resident from a rehoming centre, who has become accustomed to a kennel routine.
- Your rescued dog may be a stray who has never been housetrained.
- Housetraining may have been poor or almost non-existent in your dog's previous home.
- The trauma of losing a home and going to a rehoming centre may have affected a dog so that he has temporarily 'forgotten' his housetraining.

Although these situations are very different, the solution is to plan a housetraining regime and stick to it. Regardless of whether you are training a puppy or an adult, the dog needs to be taken out at regular intervals until he understands what is required.

Start by selecting a toilet area in your garden, and always take your dog out to this patch when you want him to perform. This will speed up the process, as your dog will quickly associate going to the toilet area with the correct response.

Give your dog a chance to have a sniff, and, when he performs, be lavish in your praise. It helps if you have a command, such as "Be clean", which you can use when your dog performs. The dog will associate the word with the action, and when you take him out, you can ask him to "Be clean". This means that you do not have to spend hours waiting for your dog, and it also means that you can take him out to "Be clean" before going to a public place where fouling would be undesirable.

When your dog has performed, have a quick game with him before going back inside. If you go in directly, the dog may adopt delaying tactics before he performs, in order to prolong his stay in the garden.

With puppies, it is easy to identify the times they should be taken out. They should go out:

- First thing in the morning
- Last thing at night
- After eating
- On waking up after a sleep
- If you see the pup sniffing or circling
- After a play session
- A minimum of every two hours.

With adult dogs, the timing may not be quite so predictable. However, as a rule of thumb, take the dog out on an hourly basis until he has learned what is required. As you get to know your dog, you can work out a routine that suits

Be patient with an adult, who may be confused as to what is required.

you both. Try to err on the side of caution; if your dog does not have the opportunity to toilet in the house, he will learn more quickly that it should take place outside.

Do not make the mistake of thinking that the dog does not need you to attend his trips out to the garden. It is much easier to let the dog out of the back door, and then call him in after a few minutes, but, in the initial stages of training, the dog *needs* to be taken to his toilet area, *he needs* to be given his command ("Be clean"), and he *needs* to be praised for performing.

INEVITABLE MISTAKES

No matter how vigilant you try to be, there will inevitably be times when the dog makes a mess in the house. First and foremost, do not be angry at the dog. The chances are that you are to blame for not seeing the signs early enough. All you can do is clean up and vow to keep a better check on your dog in the future.

When you clean up, make sure you use a deodoriser, otherwise the dog will detect the scent, and he may decide to use the spot again.

CAUGHT IN THE ACT

There is nothing to be gained from reprimanding a dog if you find a mess in the house. The 'accident' could well have happened some time previously, and the dog will not understand why you are angry (see pages 71-72). But what if you catch the dog red-handed?

You will find it almost impossible not to shout – but try to stop yourself getting irate. The dog will associate your anger with the business of performing – rather than working out that it is the place you are objecting to. The danger is that the dog will become confused and decide he should not perform while you are present – and that means all the work you have done to date will break down. This may well happen if you have a nervous dog who is upset by the trauma of settling into a new home.

If you catch your dog in the act, simply take him outside, go to his toilet area, and give the command "Be clean". In this way, the dog will learn that he must perform only in his designated area. Remember to be lavish in your praise every time your dog responds correctly.

A LESSON LEARNT

Over a period of time, your dog will become fully housetrained, and he may even get to the stage of asking to be let out. However, it is important not to be in too much of a hurry to relax your efforts in this department. Even if your dog understands what is required, he may still need you to do the thinking for him – i.e. taking him out at regular intervals. It is far better to keep up a housetraining routine for a little longer, rather than allowing accidents to happen.

THE FIRST NIGHT

This can be a traumatic moment for dog and owner alike. The dog is just beginning to settle and relax in his new surroundings, and then everyone leaves him on his own.

Difficult though it is, this is a time to make rules and stick to them. It is better not to allow a dog to sleep on your bed, or even in your bedroom. It tends to make a dog over-

A pup will be bewildered when he is left alone the first night, but he will soon learn that you will be there the next morning to greet him!

dependent, and there are also hygiene issues. In most cases, a dog that is left on his own will fret to begin with, but when he understands that barking and whining get him nowhere, he will learn to settle. Puppies can be very persistent in their protests, as they have the added trauma of being separated from their littermates for the first time. But as long as the pup is safely confined and cannot get up to any mischief, it is best to ignore his cries.

In the morning the pup (and older dog) will be delighted to see you, and will realise that the separation is only temporary, and you are on hand to serve breakfast first thing in the morning!

CHAPTER FIVE

CARING FOR YOUR DOG

When your dog arrives in his new home, you are responsible for all his needs. You will need to start work on a programme of training (see Chapter Six), and Socialisation (see Chapter Seven), but you also need to cater for his physical requirements.

THE RIGHT DIET

The best plan is to seek advice from staff at the rehoming centre, who will tell you what they have been feeding your dog. To begin with, it is important to stick to the same diet in order to avoid stomach upsets. This will also give you the chance to see if the food suits your dog. A dog should:

• Show a good appetite.
• Have no problem passing stools.
• Show no signs of diarrhoea.

If you have problems getting a particular product, or if the diet appears to be unsuitable, you can try another diet. It may be a good idea to seek advice from the vet before doing this.

Any change of diet should be made over a period of days, adding increasing amounts of the new diet, whilst decreasing the amounts of his usual food, until the transition is complete. This will give the dog's digestive system a chance to adapt.

FADDY FEEDERS

Some dogs eat with relish, and have never been known to refuse a bowl of food. Others tend to be more picky, and there are some that are downright faddy.

If your dog is continually leaving his food, try the following:

• Get the dog checked over by a vet to ensure there is no physical problem.
• Try making the food more tempting. If you are feeding a complete diet, try soaking it in gravy, or adding a little chicken to encourage the dog to eat.
• Consider a change of diet.

Some dogs are skilled in the art of begging!

be able to feel his ribs and his spine, but they should not be prominent. If you have any doubts as to whether your dog is the correct weight, ask your vet.

- Weigh your dog (your vet will have weighing scales), and then work out how much food he needs per day. Feeding guidelines will be provided by the food manufacturer, or you can ask your vet for advice.
- If you are using treats for training, deduct them from your dog's daily ration.
- Weigh your dog at regular intervals to ensure he is keeping in trim.

Beware of being too sympathetic with your dog's food fads, or you will end up continually searching for delicacies to tempt his appetite. The dog will be quick to see that he is on to a good thing, and will become increasingly fussy.

There is nothing like healthy competition to get a dog to eat. If you have another dog, or you have a friend that has a dog of impeccable temperament, try feeding the two dogs together. The faddy feeder will soon realise that he needs to eat up – fast!

AVOIDING OBESITY

Dogs are hugely skilled in the art of begging – and it can be hard to resist those big brown eyes, and that soulful expression. However, too many treats, or feeding too much at mealtimes, is a mistaken kindness. An overweight dog will suffer from a variety of health problems, as well as being too lethargic to enjoy life. You should

HANDLING

Staff at the rehoming centre will have handled your dog, and he will have been groomed regularly. It is important to continue this regime when your dog arrives in his new home. If you examine your dog on a regular basis, you will be able to spot signs of soreness, cuts, unexplained lumps, or anything else out of the ordinary. It is also important that the dog (or puppy) accepts all-over handling.

- Start by stroking your dog along the length of his body.
- As he relaxes, keep moving your hand so that you run it along the length of his tail.
- Pick up each paw and examine the pads for cuts or cracks. Check that the nails are not too long (see opposite).
- Hold the dog's head steady, and check that his eyes are clear and bright, and free from discharge. Also check that the nose is free from discharge.

A dog should get used to all-over handling.

• Look into the ears – they should be clean, with no evidence or soreness or bad odour.
• Open the dog's mouth to see if the teeth need cleaning (page 60) and check that the gums are not sore or inflamed.
• Lift the dog's tail, and check the anus is clean and the genital area looks clean and healthy.
• Ask the dog to go into the Down position, and roll him over on to his side so you can check his undercarriage. If you have a small dog, you can let the dog lie in your lap, which will make the task easier.

NAIL TRIMMING

Unless your dog exercises regularly on hard surfaces, you will need to trim his nails. You can use a nail file, but this is pretty time-consuming. Once you have learnt to use nail-clippers, you will find that these do the job quickly and effectively.

The aim is to cut the tip of the nail, so you do not catch the quick, which will bleed profusely and will hurt your dog. In white nails, you can see the quick, but if your dog has dark nails, it is

always better to err on the side of caution. If you are worried about trimming nails, ask the vet, or a nurse at the veterinary practice, to show you what to do.

Some dogs dislike having their nails trimmed, or it may be that your dog is not used to having a manicure. If this is the case, try the following:

• Recruit a helper to restrain the dog so that he does not wriggle. The helper can be armed with treats to distract the dog's attention.
• Start by lifting the dog's paw (you can give a command – "Paw"), and then praise and reward the dog for co-operating.
• Progress to fingering each nail in turn, again praising and rewarding the dog.
• Show the dog the nail-clippers, and let him sniff them. Then start the task of trimming. When the dog co-operates, be quick to praise and reward him.

If you are tactful in your handling, a dog will soon get used to having his nails trimmed.

Do not be too ambitious to begin with. The aim is to get the dog used to having his nails clipped, rather than doing a perfect job on all four feet. If you feel that your dog is getting restless, do one foot, and attend to the other feet over the next few days. If you are patient and tactful in your handling, the dog will soon get used to the routine.

TEETH CLEANING

Most dogs are fed a soft diet, and this means that teeth do not stay clean naturally. If you give your dog a marrow bone (under supervision), it will certainly help, but you will also need to clean your dog's teeth two or three times a week.

Most dogs get used to this attention without too much fuss. If your dog is sensitive about having his mouth handled, proceed in easy stages, as you did for nail trimming. Again, it may help if you recruit a helper, so you do not have to engage in a struggle.

Teeth should be cleaned on a routine basis.

- Get some treats at the ready, and start by stroking your dog around the muzzle area.
- Use a command, such as "Teeth", and open the dog's mouth. Do not be tentative; the dog is more likely to co-operate if you are purposeful in your handling. Reward the dog when he obliges.
- If your dog is not too happy about the procedure, practise opening his mouth a few more times, and leave it there.
- The next step is to open the dog's mouth and just rub a little toothpaste on his teeth. You can do this with your finger if you think he will be wary of a toothbrush. A finger brush can also be used. Again, reward the dog if he allows you to proceed.
- Most dogs like the taste of doggie toothpaste, and so once the dog has got used to sitting still while you brush, you should have few problems. Finish the session with lots of praise, and reward the dog with a treat or a game.

GROOMING

The amount of grooming your dog requires depends on his coat type. But even if you have chosen a low-maintenance breed, you must establish a regular grooming routine. This enables you to keep a close check on the dog, and it will also keep the coat in tip-top condition.

SMOOTH-COATED

The short, smooth-coated breeds and breed types are the easiest to care for. These include Greyhounds, Labrador Retrievers, Boxers, the Mastiff breeds, Rottweilers and Dobermanns.

Some terriers, such as the Staffordshire Bull Terrier and the Bull Terrier, are smooth-coated, and some Collies also have this coat type.

All that is required is regular brushing with a bristle brush. A hound glove can be used to bring out the shine in the coat, and to remove dead hair during shedding.

MEDIUM-LENGTH COAT WITH FEATHERING

All the Spaniels breeds, Golden Retrievers, Flat Coated Retrievers, and Border Collies/Working Sheepdogs share this coat type.

Regular brushing with a bristle brush or a slicker brush is required, but you will also need to comb the coat. Mats and tangles form in the feathering unless the coat is combed through. If you find a mat, you will need to tease it out with your fingers before using the comb.

HARSH-COATED

Some types of Lurcher have a harsh texture to their coat – this is often referred to as rough-coated. The Schnauzer breeds have a harsh, wiry coat, and many of the terrier breeds – the Border Terrier, some Jack Russells, the West Highland White and the Cairn Terrier – share this coat type.

In the case of the Lurcher, all you need to do is groom regularly with a slicker brush, which helps to remove dead hair. The coat will then need to be combed through. This will maintain the coat of the terrier and Schnauzer breeds, but they also need to have the coat stripped between two and four times a year to remove the dead hair. Unless you plan to become an accomplished home groomer, this will involve a trip to a professional dog groomer.

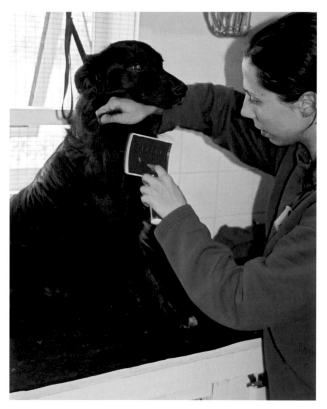

Dogs with feathering need regular grooming to prevent mats and tangles forming.

LONG-COATED

Dogs with long coats are beautiful to look at, but they are hard work! Some long-coated dogs have a shaggy, harsh-textured coat, such as the Old English Sheepdog; others have long, flowing coats, such as the Yorkshire Terrier, the Shih Tzu, and the Lhasa Apso.

If you want to keep your dog in full coat, you will need to have lengthy, daily grooming sessions. The coat needs brushing through, layer by layer with a bristle brush, and then it needs to be combed. You may also need to trim the coat in order to keep the dog clean and comfortable. For example, you may need to trim

There are some dogs that will need to be groomed every day in order to keep the coat in good order.

the hair around the anus, or cut back the hair that grows between the pads of the feet.

If you do not have the time to spend on grooming, you can take your dog to a professional groomer for a pet trim. Although the dog will not have such a spectacular coat, he can still look very smart, and the coat will be far easier to maintain.

NON-SHEDDING COATS

Poodles do not shed their coats, and so this breed can be ideal for owners with allergy problems. Routine brushing and combing is all that is required to keep the coat in order, but regular trips to the professional groomer – every eight to ten weeks – are needed so the dog can be clipped.

GROOMING AVERSION

Most dogs are perfectly happy to be groomed, particularly if they have been accustomed to the routine since puppyhood. However, there are some dogs that hate being groomed. This could be because the dog is simply not used to being handled, or more often, because the coat has been allowed to mat and tangle, and the dog has come to associate grooming with pain and discomfort.

Specialist staff at the rehoming centre bath and groom all the dogs that come in for rehoming. This is generally a straightforward business. But if the dog has been neglected, the groomer may have to spend a long time working through the coat, scissoring out the mats. Sometimes the coat is in such poor condition that it has to be clipped. It is little wonder that a dog in this situation develops an aversion to grooming.

Before the dog is rehomed, staff will have started work on overcoming the problem, but you will need to be extra sensitive in your handling until the dog learns to accept grooming as routine.

- Find a comfortable place for grooming. You may prefer to work at ground level, or you may find it less back-breaking if the dog is on a table. If you opt for a table, use a non-slip rubber mat, so the dog feels safe and secure.
- Start off by stroking the dog and handling him all over (see page 58). Make sure you have some treats to hand so you can reward him. If your dog is restless, keep the session short, and end on a positive note so that you can praise him for his good behaviour.

With patience, your dog will learn to overcome his aversion to grooming.

- Next time, introduce the brush. Let your dog sniff it, so that he realises it is not scary, and then just lay it on his coat. Give lots of verbal praise, and reward the dog.
- Progress to giving a few strokes with the brush. Concentrate on a non-sensitive area, such as along the back, so that it feels just as if you are stroking the dog. Reward him.
- At every grooming session, up the ante by asking a little more of the dog. For example, keep on brushing for a little longer, or try brushing in a more sensitive area, such as behind his ears. Give lots of verbal praise, and reward the dog at the end of a session. After a period of keeping still, he may appreciate a game.
- If you need to use the comb on your dog, wait until he is completely relaxed about being brushed. Be very careful with the comb, making sure you do not pull the hair.

Although you will be keen to have your dog looking in top condition, do not rush the stages of the exercises outlined above. It is far better to progress slowly, so that the dog accepts the attention bit by bit, rather than becoming confrontational.

BATHING

If a dog is bathed too frequently, he loses the natural oils from his coat. Generally, a bath twice a year should suffice with most dogs, but there may be times in-between – if the dog has rolled in something obnoxious – when you will need to take action! In some cases, you may be able to sponge off the dirt, but there are times when only a bath will do.

- If you have not bathed your dog before, recruit a helper so that one person can concentrate on holding on to the dog, while the other does the bathing.
- Depending on the size of the dog (and your facilities) the dog can be bathed in a sink, in a bath, or in a shower cubicle. If you are using a bath or a sink, fit a shower appliance to the taps, so that you can apply lukewarm water. You will also need to use a rubber mat so the dog does not slip.
- Groom the dog before bathing. If you have a feathered or long-coated dog, make sure the coat is free from mats and tangles.
- Soak the coat in lukewarm water, and then apply the shampoo (which should be designed for dogs). Work into a rich lather.
- Now soak the coat again, making sure you remove all traces of shampoo.
- Before the dog leaps to freedom, try to absorb as much moisture as you can with towels. If you have a long-coated dog, do not rub the coat or it will tangle.
- Allow the dog to have a good shake, and then apply more dry towels. If you have a hair-dryer, you can dry the coat, making sure the setting is low to moderate.

EXERCISE

Before adopting your dog, you will have considered the amount of exercise he will require (see page 25). Remember that exercise also provides mental stimulation, giving your dog a chance to sniff and to see new sights, so a simple route march will not be satisfactory. Obviously exercise needs will vary enormously depending on the type and age of the dog. However, it is worth bearing the following points in mind:

- Try to stick to a routine, so that the dog knows when to expect his walks. This will also mean that he is more settled in the house, as he will not feel the need to pester you.
- If you have a puppy who is still growing, limit exercise, and make sure he does not jump in and out of the car. This applies particularly to large breeds, who could damage their joints, but care should be taken with all dogs during the vulnerable growing period.
- When possible, vary the routes you take to give the dog variety.
- Do not let the dog off-lead unless you are confident that he has a reliable recall. Always check the area to make sure you are not too close to roads.
- If you have a small dog, do not ignore his exercise needs. He does not have to go for miles, but he will relish the opportunity to get out and about.
- If you have an energetic dog, remember that mental stimulation works just as well as physical exercise. Play games of retrieve or work at some training exercises, so that the dog has something to think about.
- Be aware of the changing needs of the dog as he gets older. Do not stop taking him out, but go for a variety of short walks to keep the dog active and alert.
- Finally, do not leave home without the means of cleaning up after your dog.

Do not let your dog off-lead until you have built up a reliable recall.

*T*here are some dogs who have very special needs. Fudge, a golden-coloured Cocker Spaniel, was the victim of a road traffic accident, which left him doubly incontinent and with no use of his back legs. His owner could not cope with his disabilities and put him up for rehoming. Tracey Rae, assistant manager at the Dogs Trust rehoming centre at Salisbury, remembers when he first arrived.

"It was only three weeks after the accident when Fudge came to the centre," said Tracey.

"He was still very scarred and fragile. The only way he could move was by dragging his back legs. His owner bought a trolley for him, and, as he got stronger, he was able to move around.

"He was only two years at the time, and our manager was determined to find a home for him. We tried everything: we advertised him in the local paper and he was featured on TV. There was a lot of interest, but everyone was put off when they discovered he was doubly incontinent.

GETTING BETTER

"We got used to coping with him at the centre, so that it became a matter of routine. As Fudge got better, he was increasingly lively, and it soon became clear that the trolley was not robust enough to stand up to a two-year-old Cocker Spaniel. My husband, Ken, is an engineer, and he reckoned he could come up with something more suitable. He designed a trolley that is fitted at the front with a harness, and allows the back legs to be stretched out behind. That

worked a lot better, and soon Fudge was tearing around.

"Despite all our efforts, there was still no one willing to adopt him. I started to think about whether I might be able to take him on. There were two things that influenced me. Firstly, I knew Fudge, and so I knew what to expect. I also had a friend who had a paraplegic dog, and I talked to her at great length. One day she said to me: 'No one is going to take on Fudge unless they love him already'. That swung it for me.

JOINING IN

"Fudge is now four years old, and he is a dog that really loves life. He's absolutely gorgeous, with the most amazing character. He can do everything that our other dogs do: he can run in the woods, climb over logs – he can even manage stairs with a bit of help.

"He has hydrotherapy once a fortnight, and it is beginning to make a difference. He will never be able to walk properly, but he can now stand for a few seconds, and sometimes he can manage a few paces.

"We have learnt to cope with his incontinence, and it is rarely a problem. Sometimes you have days when you think: 'What have I taken on?', but mostly it is fine.

"We now have six dogs at home – and all of them are rescued dogs. We have Ross, a Collie cross, whom we rehomed as a pup. He is now 14 years old, but he is still the leader. Merlin is a beautiful, big Lurcher. We think he is probably a Deerhound/German Shepherd cross. He is ten years old, and although he can be quite

Continued on page 67

Fudge: Living life to the full! He can do everything that the other dogs do, including giving them a run for their money!

Fudge is one of the pack, and he is accepted by all the other dogs.

Continued from page 65
feisty, he also has a gentle side to his character.

"We also have Kirk, a nine-year-old German Shepherd/Ridgeback cross. He was in kennels for five years before we rehomed him. I have no idea why he was left for so long, because we have never had any problems with him.

SIGN LANGUAGE

"We adopted Hope, a German Shepherd/ Dobermann cross, knowing she was totally deaf. We use sign language with her, and the other dogs have picked it up.

"We did have some issues with Hope to begin with. For example, she was not trustworthy with people. However, we have worked hard with her, and she is now a totally different dog.

"Our youngest dog is Penny, whom we adopted when she was just three months old. We think she is a mixture of German Shepherd, Rough Collie and Corgi. She's about knee-high, and she's a beautiful dog.

PLACE IN THE PACK

"We are lucky that all our dogs get on well together – all six of them! Fortunately, they all know their places in the pack, so we have few arguments. The dogs are all such different characters – and we love them all in their different ways."

CHAPTER SIX

TRAINING TARGETS

Before adopting a rescued dog, you probably envisaged the type of companion you would like, and what level of training you wanted your dog to achieve.

- You may be content with a well-behaved family dog with a basic level of obedience.
- You may have ambitions to compete in one of the canine disciplines, such as Competitive Obedience or Agility (see pages 86-91).
- You may be taking on the challenge of a rescued dog who has specific problems to overcome (see Chapter Eight).
- Perhaps you have adopted a puppy, and you have to start training from scratch.

In all cases, your chances of success will be greatly increased if you have an understanding of how your dog's mind works. Every breed has certain in-bred characteristics that will influence its behaviour (see Chapter One), and every individual is different, but the same broad principles will apply regardless of whether you are adopting a Yorkshire Terrier, a Great Dane, or a Heinz 57.

LEADERSHIP

Dogs are descended from wolves, and despite thousands of years of domestication, they still have close links with their wolf ancestry. This is good news for human owners, as the dog is ready to accept leadership.

In order to achieve a balanced relationship, you do not need to be a strict disciplinarian who treats the dog as a lowly, inferior creature. Just establish a code of behaviour that your dog understands – and stick to it. In this way, your dog will know where he stands without constantly being nagged at. You do not have to bark out orders. Dogs have an excellent sense of hearing, and a few well-chosen words, coupled with lots of praise when your dog co-operates, will be far more effective.

COMMUNICATING

Although we do not share a verbal language,

A dog will read a lot from our body language.

there are ways of communicating and picking up on signals so that both dog and handler understand each other.

BODY LANGUAGE

This is vitally important in the animal kingdom, although we humans tend to give it scant regard. If you watch any animal, you can find out a great deal about how they are feeling simply by watching their body posture, their gestures, and their facial expressions (see pages 103-105).

While we are observing the dog to understand his feelings, he will be looking at us and interpreting our body language. This is a subtle art, which we cannot wholly fathom. It is well

known that a dog will pick up on his owner's mood, even though we do not think we have shown any change in our behaviour. A dog seems to know if we are upset or depressed, or in the mood for fun.

On a more basic level, we can use body language as an aid to training. For example:

- If you want your dog to come to you, open your arms so that you appear open and welcoming.
- If you want your dog to stay, keep your body still and use a handsignal – palm flat, held towards the dog.
- To ignore undesirable behaviour, avoid eye contact and turn your back on your dog.

- If you have a timid dog, do not stand over him when you give commands – this makes you appear threatening.

As you get to know your dog, and you advance further in your training, you can fine-tune your body language so that the dog picks up on the tiniest of signals. This is the secret behind the success of top trainers in all the canine disciplines.

TONE OF VOICE

A dog does not understand the words we use, but he does understand the tone of voice. This can be one of the most useful tools when it comes to training.

- A deep, gruff voice should be used when you are reprimanding your dog. You do not have to shout or confuse your dog with too many words. For example, a stern "No" or "Leave" will be far more effective than: "Oh, Prince, you bad dog, you mustn't do that!"
- Praise should be given in a warm, encouraging tone of voice so that your dog knows that you are pleased with him.
- When training, sound bright and positive, and keep your voice up-beat so that the dog is motivated to listen to you. If you sound dull and boring, it will be little wonder if the dog switches off.

ASSOCIATION

A dog learns by association. For example, a dog learns to Sit when we give that command – not because he understands the meaning of the word, but because he understands that a Sit is the correct response to the sound you are making. If you started from scratch and said "Bananas" rather than "Sit", he would learn to Sit on that command instead!

To facilitate quick learning, commands should be simple and consistent. You know what you want when you say: "Prince, Down, Lie Down, Get Down," but this jumble of words is confusing to a dog. A simple "Prince, Down" will be far more effective.

TIMING

This is closely linked to the concept of association. A dog learns to associate a command with an action, but only if you get the timing right.If you teach your dog to Sit using a treat (see page 77), he is being lured into the correct position. You need to add the command "Sit" as soon as he responds correctly, and he will form an association between the command and the action. However, if you keep saying "Sit" when your dog is still standing, or "Sit" when he breaks the position, he will not make the link.

In the early stages of training, only use commands when your dog is doing what you want, and then praise him lavishly so that he understands he is doing the right thing. Make sure praise is given the instant your dog has responded correctly.

The same principle applies to punishing your dog. A dog's association time between the action he has committed is fleeting – literally a matter of seconds. If your dog has done something wrong, you must catch him red-handed or he will have no idea why you are displeased. People often say a dog looks guilty when he is being told off for a crime that was committed hours previously. But, in fact, the dog is merely responding to your angry tone of voice. He has no idea why you are angry with him – and he will certainly not learn anything from his telling off. In his mind, he came up to greet you, and he was immediately punished. You can see the evidence of the crime – a raided bin, or a chewed-up slipper – but as far as the dog is concerned, he is being told off for coming up to greet you.

Difficult though it may be on some occasions, try to curb your frustration, and work on preventing problems from arising. If your dog does not have access to a bin when he is left alone, and if you tidy away valuables, it will lessen his opportunities for undesirable behaviour. This means that when you come home and the dog has done nothing wrong, you can be genuinely pleased to see him – and the dog will feel increasingly secure and confident in his new home.

MOTIVATION

Generally, dogs are eager to please their human owners, but there are times when their own agenda is more pressing. For example, it is far more rewarding for a dog to run off with a playmate rather than respond to your recall command. There are also times when you are trying to teach a new exercise. Most dogs will quickly lose interest unless there is a reason – a reward to work for.

Verbal praise and stroking are excellent ways of rewarding your dog, but if you want your dog to go that extra mile – focusing on a new training exercise, or coming back to you in the park – you will need something extra. Your task is to find out what motivates your dog.

FOOD REWARDS

Most dogs will work for food treats. The real foodies of the canine world will be happy with any type of food treat, but those that are more picky will work better if you provide a really tasty reward. This could be cheese, sausage, or cooked liver. In most cases, the smellier the treat, the more the dog likes it! Experiment with your dog and find out what is his particular favourite.

You can use these special treats for training sessions, or you may find it more effective if you vary the diet. You can use shop-bought treats (which are easier to handle) on a regular basis, and reserve the special treats for more challenging occasions, such as when you are working on a new exercise or for recalls away from home.

COUNTING CALORIES

It is important that your dog does not get more food than he needs because you are using treats. The best plan is to weigh out the treats you are using each day, and then subtract this amount from your dog's food ration.

TOY REWARDS

There are some dogs who are toy mad, and a game will be considered a greater reward than food. Border Collies and Working Sheepdogs tend to be very toy-orientated; for this type of dog, you will need to find a special training toy. It doesn't matter what it is – a tug toy, a squeaky toy or a ball – but it must be something

Most dogs will be happy to work for food treats (left). Others prefer a game with a favourite toy (right).

that your dog really wants. Keep this toy to one side and produce it for training sessions. This gives the toy added value, and your dog will be motivated to work hard so that he gets his reward – a game with his favourite toy.

EXPECTATIONS

Before you plan a training programme, you should work out what you want to achieve and what you think your dog is capable of achieving.

BREED TYPE

There is no doubt that some breeds are easier to train than others (see Chapter One). For example:

- Border Collie and Collie types are quick to learn, and thrive on the challenge of training.
- Greyhounds and Lurchers have a more placid, laid-back temperament, and will take training at their own pace.
- Terriers have an independent spirit, and you will need to focus their attention.
- The Retriever breeds, such as Labradors and Golden Retrievers, are eager to please, but need firm handling.
- German Shepherds and Shepherd types are often very sensitive, requiring tactful handling.

AGE

Age also plays a part in deciding what your dog is capable of. If you have a puppy or a young

The clicker is used to mark correct behaviour – which you then reward.

Clicker training is a relatively new way of training, which was pioneered by Karen Pryor when she was working with dolphins in the USA. She has adapted clicker training, and it has proved highly successful with dogs, cats, horses, and even fish!

A clicker is a small, plastic box. It fits comfortably in the hand, and makes a distinctive 'click' when pressed with the thumb. The click is best described as a 'yes' marker, telling your dog he has done something that pleases you. As soon as you click, follow it up with a reward, and, in no time, your dog will associate the sound of the click with getting a reward.

The major advantage of the clicker is that it marks correct behaviour at the precise moment that it happens. The dog does not have to wait to be praised or given a reward after the exercise is finished, which often confuses the issue. He is clicked the moment he is responding correctly, and he is in no doubt that he is doing what you want. This precise timing can be very useful when you are training a rescued dog who may, initially, be perplexed about what you are asking him to do, and will benefit from the reassurance of knowing he is getting it right.

It takes a bit of practice to get used to using a clicker and getting your timing right. You may find it helpful to find a training club that specialises in clicker training (see page 85) so that expert instructors can give you a helping hand.

dog, you can start with a fresh sheet and teach him as much as you want. An older dog will be more set in his ways, and although you certainly can teach an old dog new tricks, you may have to work harder at motivating your dog so that he is keen to co-operate with you.

TEMPERAMENT

You also need to assess your dog's individual temperament and tailor your training accordingly.

- If you have a nervous dog, your main aim is to boost his confidence to make him feel safe and secure. Set training targets that are easy to attain so that you can give your dog lots of praise. Progress in easy stages, and do not overtax your dog during his settling-in period.

- If you have an excitable dog, keep training low-key, giving out lots of calming signals. Keep your body as still as possible, and although you need to change your tone of voice for praise, do not get the dog hyped up. This type of dog often offers lots of different behaviours when you are training. He may jump up at you when you are training him to Sit, or he may start barking or whining in the middle of an exercise. This is an attention-seeking device, and the best policy is to ignore the behaviour you do not want, and praise the behaviour that you have asked for.

- A sensitive dog may be very clingy and need a lot of reassurance. He may have suffered abuse or neglect in his previous home, and no longer trusts people. Again, make training easy so that you can give lots of praise. Adopt a kind, matter-of-fact manner, so that your dog begins to relax in your presence.

- Some dogs have been through so much that they simply switch off and become very unresponsive. This can also happen if a dog has been in kennels for a long time, and has become 'institutionalised'. With this type of dog you need to work on motivation – finding a reward that he really rates – and do not be too demanding in your training programme.

GETTING STARTED

The first training target should be set before your dog arrives in his new home. You, and your family, need to decide on a set of house rules, and then pledge to be consistent in carrying them out. You cannot expect a dog to learn if you allow him on the sofa one day, and

Set realistic expectations as to what you can achieve with your dog.

then are furious the next time he does it because he has muddy feet. As far as the dog is concerned, he has behaved in exactly the same way on both occasions, and your anger and disapproval are inexplicable. From the dog's viewpoint, this looks like weak leadership, and he will start to lose respect for you.

The type of house rules you should consider are:

- Is the dog allowed to sleep on the bed?
- Is the dog allowed to climb on to the furniture?
- Is the dog allowed upstairs?
- Is the dog allowed to jump up when he greets people?
- Is the dog allowed to beg when you are eating?
- Do you mind if the dog pushes through doorways ahead of you?

To a large extent, the rules you lay down are a matter of personal preference. However, if you have a dog with dominant tendencies (see page 105) you need to be aware of the consequences of your actions. This type of dog is seeking to test the limits, and it is better not to give him the opportunity to increase his status.

ENFORCING THE RULES

If you are taking on a puppy, it is a relatively easy matter to set house rules and then enforce them. The pup comes to everything fresh. He has no history, and therefore he is prepared to accept the status quo without question, as long as you are firm and consistent.

When you adopt an older dog, in most cases you simply do not know what you are taking on.

• You may have a well-trained dog who is familiar with living in a family and abiding by the rules.

• You may have a stray dog who has never lived in a home.
• You may have an ex-racing Greyhound who is only used to living in kennels.
• You may have a dog that has been given no training and has become hard to handle.
• You may have a dog that has suffered cruelty or neglect, whose understanding of home life will be very distorted.
• You may have adopted a long-stay resident at the rehoming centre, who has forgotten what family life is like.

If your dog is not used to a home environment, or has no perception of how to behave in a family home, you need to go back to basics and treat the dog like a puppy. There is no point in shouting at the dog because he leaps on the sofa or he jumps up to steal some food from the table. He has no moral sense that he is doing wrong – he is simply exploiting the opportunities that present themselves.

Try to spend as much time as possible with your dog so that you can supervise his behaviour. You may find it helpful to use a stair-gate so that you can block off the upstairs of the house, or to confine him to a couple of rooms.

When the dog does something undesirable, such as climbing on to a chair, be quick and firm in your response. Tell him "No" in a deep, firm voice, and then call him to you. When the dog responds, reward him with a treat. In this way, the dog will learn that if responds to you, he will be rewarded. Obviously, the dog will try

A newly adopted dog needs to learn what is acceptable behaviour in your home.

to get on the furniture again, but if you react in the same way every time, he will get the message.

BASIC EXERCISES

The amount of work you need to do on basic training exercises will vary enormously depending on the dog you have adopted. However, it is generally a good idea to start from scratch so that you can see what your dog knows. It is always better to be able to reward a dog for doing something well, even though it may be as simple as a Sit, and then you create a positive learning environment.

A puppy has a very short concentration span, and the secret of training is little and often. Exactly the same applies when you are training a rescued dog, even though he may be fully mature. A rescued dog has so many anxieties to cope with as he settles into a new home that his mind is already brimful. It is therefore important not to overtax your dog in the first few weeks. Keep things simple, and be lavish in your praise and your rewards.

Choose a training environment that is as free from distractions as possible This means that the dog will have no option but to focus on you, which will make training easier. As the dog progresses, you can be more ambitious and progress from the hall to the garden, for example, to give the dog a greater challenge.

The exercises outlined below are based on positively reinforcing correct behaviour with praise and reward. You need to decide the type of reward that works best for your dog. If you plan to use a clicker (see page 74), remember to click when your dog responds correctly, and

follow it up with a reward when the exercise is finished.

KEEP IT POSITIVE

If, at any time, your dog is struggling to master an exercise, do not give way to frustration. The dog will pick up on your negativity, and will become even more confused. He may even start to dread his training sessions.

If a problem arises that is not easy to solve, forget it, and revert to an exercise that you know the dog is happy with. This will give you the opportunity to praise and reward the dog, and you can end the training session on a positive note.

You may well find that when you try the exercise on another occasion, the dog will be more responsive, as he will not feel under pressure.

SIT

This is the simplest exercise to teach, and so you can start your training programme on a positive note with success guaranteed.

• Show your dog that you have a treat in your hand, and then hold it above his nose, just out of reach.
• As the dog looks up at the treat, he will lower his hindquarters, and hopefully go into the Sit.
• As the dog goes into the Sit, give the command "Sit", and then praise and reward him.

Practise this a few times, and your dog will quickly get the idea. You can also train the Sit at

Start by teaching the Sit – and you will be rewarded with almost instant success.

- When you have your dog's attention, lower your hand to the ground. Your dog will follow the lure, maybe crouching down on his forequarters.
- Keep your fist closed over the treat, and as the dog tries to get at it, he will lower his hindquarters, going into the Down position.
- As he goes into the Down, give the command "Down", then praise and reward.
- If your dog is struggling, you can apply light pressure to his shoulders to encourage him to go into position.
- Practise a few times, gradually extending the time your dog stays in the Down.

With practice, you will be able to give the command "Down" while standing upright rather than having to lure your dog into position.

mealtimes, asking your dog to "Sit" before you put down his bowl.

Note: Greyhounds, and some of the other tall sighthound breeds, find the Sit an uncomfortable position to adopt. You can ask your dog to Sit for just a few moments, but if he is clearly upset, do not force the issue.

DOWN

This is a useful exercise to teach, as it can be used to encourage your dog to settle for longer periods.

- Show the dog that you have a treat, and then close your fist over it.

Use a treat to lure your dog into the Down.

STAND

This is an optional exercise in the sense that you can get by quite easily without it. However, it can come in handy when you are grooming, or if the vet needs to examine your dog.

- Use a treat and hold it just out of your dog's reach. Stroke along your dog's tummy, so that he does not go into the Sit or the Down but reaches out to get the treat.
- Repeat the exercise, saying "Stand" when your dog is in the correct position.
- Keep on practising, as it takes a little time for the dog to understand what you want.
- Gradually increase the length of time your dog is in the Stand, and then give lots of praise and a reward.

LEAD-TRAINING

A source of trouble for many owners! The best plan is to work at this exercise in short bursts, concentrating on the dog, rather than trying to combine a training session with a shopping trip.

FOR PUPPIES

If you have a puppy, you will need to start lead-training from scratch.

- First, the pup must get used to wearing a collar. Choose a light, adjustable collar, and fit it just before a meal. The pup will be so interested in eating his food, he will not notice that he is wearing a collar.
- Once the pup has finished eating, he may scratch his collar. Again, distract his attention, this time with a game. Keep the collar on for short periods until the pup gets used to it.
- Now attach the lead. Allow the pup to walk around with the lead trailing, making sure he does not get tangled up.
- Take hold of the lead and follow the pup wherever he goes.
- For the next step, you will need some treats or a toy. Hold the lead in one hand and show the pup the treats/toy in your other hand. Use your puppy's name and encourage him to walk with you. After a few steps, praise him

Use a treat or a toy to encourage a pup to walk to heel.

THE LAGGING DOG

Above: Sometimes a dog will put on the brakes and refuse to move. Right: Avoid a battle of wills by using a treat to motivate the dog to come towards you.

THE PULLING DOG

If you have a dog that pulls, you must offer an incentive so the dog refocuses his attention on you.

and give him his reward.

- Introduce the command "Heel" or "Close" when your pup is walking by your side. Make sure you only use the command when the pup is in the correct position.
- Over a period of time, build up lead-training so that your pup walks to heel in a circle, and takes on board changes of direction. Remember to give lots of praise, and reward at frequent intervals.

FOR OLDER DOGS

The dog you have adopted may be used to walking on the lead, and so you will not have too much work to do on this aspect of his training. Ex-racing Greyhounds are accustomed to lead-walking, and new owners often get a nice surprise when they discover they can walk their Greyhound on a loose lead.

However, you may well find that your dog is used to the lead but he has developed bad habits.

THE LAGGING DOG

A dog that stops and sniffs at every lamp-post and blade of grass can be annoying, but it is a problem that is easy to solve.

- To begin with, only take your dog out on the lead when you are going somewhere pleasurable, such as the park. In this way, the dog will associate the lead with something that he likes, and he will set off in a positive frame of mind.
- Arm yourself with some tasty treats, so that if your dog stops to sniff, you can attract his attention and offer him a more attractive alternative.

- Remember to give the command "Heel" or "Close" when the dog is walking nicely by your side, and praise him for his co-operation. Make sure you sound bright and positive so that your dog will want to walk with you.
- If you achieve a reasonable stretch of good heelwork, reward your dog with a treat so that he has an incentive to keep on walking with you.
- Do not use the "Heel"/"Close" command when your dog has stopped in order to try to encourage him to come to heel. The dog will fail to associate the command with the behaviour you want.
- Introduce changes of direction and pace to make lead-walking more interesting. It will keep the dog on his toes, trying to anticipate what you are going to do next.

As your dog becomes more settled and starts to respect and trust you, he will become more eager to please. Be consistent in your training, so that your dog does not get away with lagging on the lead. Keep a supply of treats with you, and, as you progress, reward the dog intermittently when he is walking nicely by your side.

THE PULLING DOG

This is a far more common problem, and it is harder to solve, particularly if the habit has become ingrained. You may consider using an anti-pulling device (see page 35) so that you have more control.

The most important point to realise is that the more you pull against your dog, the more he will pull. Some dogs seem to relish squaring up their shoulders and pulling as hard as they can, and so you must put a stop to this scenario right from the start.

- Before you attempt lead-training, have a game with your dog, or let him have some free-running exercise so that he gets rid of some energy.
- Arm yourself with some tasty treats, or a toy if that works better for your dog. Choose a location that is as free from distractions as possible to give the best chance of success.
- Walk a few paces, and the second your dog surges ahead, stop. Call your dog to you, and reward him with a treat or a quick game with his toy.
- Get your dog back by your side (traditionally dogs are trained to walk to heel on the handler's left side), and proceed for a few more paces.
- Repeat the exercise as above, rewarding your dog when the lead goes slack and he focuses on you. The aim is for the dog to realise that a slack lead means nice things, and pulling gets him nowhere.
- When you get a few paces of good heelwork, be quick to use the command "Heel"/"Close" and give lots of praise so that your dog is in no doubt that this is the correct position to be in. Give a reward when you are on the move – as long as the dog is in the correct position – so the dog is motivated to stay at your side.
- When your dog understands what you want and is walking to heel and focusing on you, it is time to introduce some distractions. Recruit a friend with a dog, and walk your dog past the other dog. If your dog pulls towards the

Use a hand signal to back up your verbal command.

other dog, stop, call him to you, and then reward him.

• You will have to work on this exercise over a period of time so that your dog realises that the best reward is staying with you, with the lead slack. It is a good idea if you can end the training sessions by letting both dogs off the lead for a play, so that your dog has a further reward for his good behaviour.

• You can also use a food bowl or a toy as 'bait'. Again, when the dog pulls towards the object of his desires, call him to you and reward him.

Patience is required to stop a dog from pulling, but if you are prepared to put in the work and you are 100 per cent consistent in your training, you will win in the end.

It may help if you enlist at a training class (see page 85) where expert instructors will be on hand to help you.

WAIT/STAY

Some handlers use "Stay" when they want their dog to maintain a position for a length of time, and use "Wait" if they want the dog to maintain position for a few moments, such as just before a recall. The dog will learn the distinction, but if you prefer, you can use the same command for both situations. They are both trained in the following way:

• Attach a lead, and ask the dog to Sit at your side. If your dog is more likely to stay in the Down, you can start with this position.

• Ask the dog to "Wait"/"Stay" and step one pace to the side. You can reinforce the command by giving a handsignal – flat hand, palm towards the dog.

• Pause a few seconds, and then step back to your dog's side. Bend down, and quietly praise and reward the dog, while he remains in the position. Keep your body language as low-key as possible, or you will encourage the dog to jump up.

• Finish the exercise by giving a release command, such as "Okay", so your dog learns that this is the signal to break position.

• Keep on practising, increasing the distance you can leave your dog.

• When your dog is maintaining position, try the exercise again, this time standing in front of the dog, and stepping one pace backwards.

Gradually increase the distance you can leave your dog.

- A dog will often break position as you return to him. To prevent this, repeat the command "Stay"/"Wait" as you approach. As he becomes more settled, you can walk a circle around him, or step over his back so that he learns he must maintain his position regardless of what you are doing. It is only when you give the release command that he is allowed to move.
- Vary the exercise by training your dog to stay in both the Sit or the Down, or, if you feel really ambitious, you can try a Stand-Stay!

As your dog grows in confidence, you will be able to give the "Stay"/"Wait" when you are at your dog's side, and you can then walk away, with your back to the dog, knowing he will still stay in position.

RECALL

There is nothing more frustrating than having a dog who is deaf to your calls – and in some situations it could lead to disastrous results.

Rehoming centres will give advice as to how long to wait before you allow your dog off the lead in a public place. At Dogs Trust, it is recommended to wait at least six weeks for the dog to be settled and to feel he is part of his new family.

However, you can use the time to advantage by practising the Recall at home before trying it for real. If you have adopted a puppy, you can use the exercises outlined below, and the pup should develop a top-class, reliable Recall.

The aim of the Recall exercise is to make yourself so attractive that your dog wants to come to you, regardless of all temptations. It would be nice to think that a dog will come to you for love alone – but most need an added incentive! This is the time to use your dog's favourite treats, or to reward him with a really good game with his toy. This will give him the motivation to come to you, as you can provide the best reward.

- Start Recall training in the house. To begin, just call the dog to you from across the room: "Prince, Come." When he comes, give lots of praise, and reward him with a treat or a game with his toy.
- Progress to calling the dog from room to room. You can call him at mealtimes, and then you can give him a bumper reward when he comes to you!
- Now try some Recalls in the garden. This is an exercise where you need to sound really exciting, so that your dog will break off from what he is doing to come to you.

Make yourself irresistible so your pup really wants to come to you.

- When your dog starts coming towards you, open your arms so that you look welcoming, and be ready with the reward. To begin with, do not worry about asking your dog to Sit when he comes to you. The aim is to build up an enthusiastic response – you can fine-tune it later on.
- If your dog is slow in coming to you, jump up and down. Don't worry about making a fool of yourself – the sillier you look, the more likely your dog is to respond!

BLOWING THE WHISTLE

You can use a whistle to help Recall training. Every time your dog has a meal, blow the whistle. Decide on the signal you want – for example, two peeps of the whistle – and stick to it. The dog will quickly learn to associate the sound of the whistle with food.

When you start Recall training, give the same whistle signal, and your dog should come hurtling towards you. Make sure you have a reward ready so that the dog knows he has responded correctly, and that the whistle means food, regardless of where he is.

Practise in the house, and then in the garden – for example, when calling your dog in from outside. Hopefully, by the time you are ready to try a Recall away from home, the dog should have built up a really strong response.

MAKE IT FUN!

All too often, a Recall signals the end of fun for a dog. It is generally used at the end of a walk,

and the dog is put back on the lead. It is no wonder that an intelligent dog decides to ignore his owner and pursue his own interests.

You can avoid this situation from arising if you do some fun exercises involving the Recall.

- Recruit a helper and take your dog into the garden. Call the dog in turn, each person rewarding the dog when he comes.
- You can extend this to playing hide-and-seek, calling the dog to you from a hiding place. The dog will enjoy seeking you out, and then you can give him a big reward when he finds you. Children can also get involved in this game (see page 46).
- When you are on a walk, call the dog to you, and reward him or have a game with a toy. The dog will learn that coming to you means fun – it is not the signal that a walk is over.

Arm yourself with a toy or some treats so that the dog is instantly rewarded for coming to you.

TRYING IT IN PUBLIC

The big test comes when you try a Recall outside the confines of your home or garden. Obviously, you will not try this until you are confident that you have built up a good response to the exercise at home.

- The first time you try to Recall away from home, it is a good idea to use a training line – a length of rope or cord 2.75-3.65 m (9-12 ft), which you can attach to your dog's collar.
- Go to the park with a helper, and attach the training line. Walk away from the dog, while the helper holds on to him until you call.
- The helper releases the dog, and, hopefully, he will come straight to you, and you can give him a big reward. However, if he has other ideas, the helper can quickly catch hold of the training line, so you do not lose control.
- Practise this exercise a few times, and the dog will learn to come running for his reward. You can then progress to trying the Recall without the training line.
- If your dog is slow in responding, try running off while the helper holds on to the dog. This will stimulate the dog to chase after you.
- You can also try turning your back and running a few paces as the dog comes in to you. This helps to motivate the dog to come in quickly, and then you can reward him.
- When your dog is responding enthusiastically to the Recall, you can introduce a Sit when the dog gets to you. This is useful for when you want to attach the lead at the end of a walk. However, do not try this too soon, or you will slow the dog's response.
- Ask the dog to "Sit", attach the lead, and then

GOLDEN RULE

Never *tell your dog off for a slow response to the Recall – no matter how frustrated you feel! It may be that your dog has stopped to investigate a smell, or has been distracted by another dog, but if he comes – albeit eventually – you must praise him. If you chastise the dog, he will think he is being told off for coming, and he certainly won't be in a hurry to come next time.*

It is essential that the dog always associates coming to you with a reward. It is a big thing to ask a dog to stop what he is doing to come to you; he needs constant motivation and reward so he is always ready to respond to you.

reward him. In this way, the dog will associate the lead being attached with getting a reward, rather than seeing it as signalling the end of his freedom.

TRAINING CLASSES

When your dog has settled in his new home, and you have started to develop a relationship with him, you may decide to enrol at a training club. This can have a number of benefits:

- You have a set period every week when you can concentrate on your dog and work at his training.
- Instructors will be on hand to help you overcome problems.
- Your dog will socialise with other dogs.
- Despite all the distractions at the training class, your dog will learn to focus on you.

Check out your local training class to ensure it uses reward-based training methods.

• You will meet like-minded doggie people and you will have the chance to exchange ideas and information.

Some rehoming centres hold training classes for newly adopted dogs. This is ideal, as the instructor will already know the dog, and will be able to give tailor-made advice. Otherwise, you will need to find a local club. First, go along to watch how the classes are run. It is best to go without your dog so you can concentrate on what is going on. Find out the following:

Is training based on positive, reward-based methods?
It is widely accepted that reward-based methods of training are not only kinder, they are also far more effective than relying on punishment. It may also be helpful if the club uses clicker training (see page 74).

Do any of the instructors have any experience with your breed/type of dog?
An instructor who knows your type of dog will have realistic expectations of his capabilities, and how to bring out the best in him.

Do any of the instructors have experience with rescued dogs?
This is not essential, but it will certainly be very useful, as the instructor will have had encountered dogs with problems that stem from having an unsettled history.

Are classes organised according to age and ability?
Youngsters can easily be frightened by large, noisy adults, and so it is preferable to have a class for puppies and a class for adults. Dogs can be taught in mixed-ability classes, but it is more rewarding for both dog and handler to work in a class that suits their standard.

SPECIALIST ACTIVITIES
If your dog is bright and intelligent, and enjoys his training, why not get involved in a sport to bring out your dog's talents? You do not have to

compete at the highest level – in fact, you don't need to compete at all if you don't want to. The aim is to have fun, to provide mental stimulation, and to enrich your relationship with your dog.

GOOD CITIZEN AWARDS

This is a scheme devised by the Kennel Club, and is now run at many training clubs. The tests are designed to create good citizens out of our dogs, and so the emphasis is on acquiring social skills (e.g. being examined and groomed, working alongside other dogs, waiting to be given food, and letting the handler walk through a door first). These exercises are suited to dogs of all ages, and so they are something to aim for if you have adopted an adult rescued dog.

The three stages – bronze, silver and gold – have an increasing level of difficulty, but all are within the compass of the average dog and handler.

COMPETITIVE OBEDIENCE

This is a precision sport, where control and accuracy are all-important. The exercises include: Heelwork (on- and off-lead), Recalls, Retrieve, Stays, Distance control, Sendaway and Scent discrimination.

If you think your dog has what it takes, you will need to find a training club that specialises in this type of advanced training.

AGILITY

Both dog and handler need to be fit to compete in Agility. It comprises an obstacle course where the dog must negotiate contact equipment (dog walk, A-frame, and see-saw), as well as tunnels (rigid and collapsible), hurdles, weaving poles,

and tyres (lollipop or set in a frame).

Speed is a must, as the dog competes against the clock, but control is also needed, as the dog is faulted for missing contact points, having poles down, missing weaving poles, and for taking the wrong course.

Dogs need to be over 12 months of age before they start training, and you will need to find a club that specialises in Agility.

WORKING TRIALS

This is a discipline that combines elements of Obedience and Agility, but there is also a large proportion of tracking. A successful Working Trials dog needs to have a good nose; he must work closely with the handler, but also have the initiative to work independently.

There are clubs that specialise in Working Trials, and there are also instructors who give one-to-one tuition.

THERAPY DOGS

This is something that dogs of any size, age or ability can get involved in. The only pre-requisite is that the dog must be sound in temperament. Therapy dogs (known as PAT dogs after the charity Pets As Therapy) go with their owners to visit residential homes for the elderly, hospitals, and other institutions where pets cannot be kept. The residents/patients derive tremendous benefit from having contact with a dog, and there is the added satisfaction of knowing that a rescued dog is doing something special in the community.

If you want to get involved in therapy work, your dog will have to undergo a temperament test to prove that he is 100 per cent reliable.

Nine years ago, Jo Bird adopted Bea, an eight-month-old Collie cross. Now, she shares her home with five rescued dogs (all from Dogs Trust) – and she has a cabinet full of trophies.

"When I first saw Bea, she looked so pathetic," said Jo. "She was not the prettiest dog, but there was something about her that was so endearing. She had been returned from her third home, and she had just about given up on people. When she was brought out of her kennel, she turned her back on me. She didn't want to know.

"I had quite a battle to get her because I was only 21 at the time, and the rehoming staff thought I was too young and inexperienced. I had grown up with dogs – mostly terriers – but I didn't know anything about Collies. I managed to persuade the staff that I could provide a good home, and even though we had some difficult times, we never looked back. There was no way I was ever going to give up on her.

"When Bea first came home, she was no hassle. I was warned that she might be destructive or hard to handle, but she was completely switched off. She was a screwed-up mess, and it was obvious that she didn't trust me. It was as if she thought that at any moment she might get dumped again. She knew absolutely nothing as far as training was concerned, and she had no idea how to play. You could throw a toy at her, and she would just look at you as if to say: 'What are you doing?'

"The biggest problem was that she was funny with other dogs. She was never nasty, but she wasn't happy if another dog came up too close.

I took her to our local dog training club, but they told me they didn't want us to join because Bea was too disobedient. That was a low spot, but I was not going to be beaten.

"At the Dogs Trust rehoming centre at Evesham, where I got Bea, they run a training club (K9 Capers) for dogs that have been adopted, as well as other dogs in the community. That was a turning point, because there were people there who understood the problems of rescued dogs and were able to give the help and support I needed.

ENTER JAKE

"By the time Bea was 18 months old, I felt I had got as far with her as I could. She was mixing with other dogs and she trusted me, but she still wouldn't play. I thought that if I had a puppy, it would bring her out of herself.

"I went back to the rehoming centre at Evesham, and they had a litter of Collie/Spaniel crosses that had been brought in suffering from parvovirus. I chose Jake, and he came home

Bea (left) needed the companionship of another dog – Jake (right) – to bring her out of herself.

when he was eight weeks old. He had recovered from the parvo, but it left him with poor sight in one eye.

"When he came home, he wanted to play with Bea. She would put up with him for so long, and then bare her teeth and walk away. Jake very quickly learnt not to follow her. He understood that he must respect her personal space. As Jake got bigger, we started playing with him, and he loved his toys. Bea used to watch, and you could see her thinking, 'That looks like fun.' At last, the penny dropped, and we got her to play. From then on, she made up for lost time, and now she is toy-mad. She goes wild for squeaky toys, and at Christmas she unwraps all the presents hoping to find one. She holds the world record for how fast she can remove the squeaker!

"Jake was the dog that got me into Agility. I took him to the Dogs Trust training club, and we did some fun Agility. He loved it, and so I joined a specialist Agility club, and he's turned out to be a real star. He has some difficulty because of the poor sight in one eye, but he's proved to be a really good, strong team dog. In 2001, we were invited to Crufts and took part in an Agility display made up of rescued dogs. They came from Dogs Trust, RSPCA, Blue Cross, Battersea Dogs' Home, and Wood Green Animal Shelter.

THE FOXY FLYER

"I wanted a Border Collie pup that I could train specifically for Agility, and I came back with something that looked like a fox! Amber is a Collie crossed with goodness knows what! She is a Golden Retriever colour, but is quite small, only

Jake in full flight over the hurdles.

18 inches at the shoulder, and she has the prettiest face. I think she may have some Shetland Sheepdog in her.

"Amber was a year old when I adopted her, and I have never known a dog to learn so fast. When I went to see her at the rehoming centre, she came out of the kennel, and within half an hour, I had taught her Sit, Down, and to walk to heel while looking at me. She was so keen to work. It was as if she was saying: 'This is the thing I most want to do.'

"When she first came home, there were some problems between her and Bea. As the two bitches in the household, they were uneasy with each other. I made the mistake of trying to intervene. I kept telling Amber to leave Bea alone. I didn't realise that, by giving Amber attention, I was undermining Bea's status as top dog.

Continued on page 90

Amber: The only trouble is keeping up with her!

Continued from page 89

"They would be okay for a couple of weeks, and then they would flare up. It was obvious that their relationship was not resolved. One day, they had a go at each other, and I decided to let them sort things out for themselves. I stood by, in case things got nasty, but it was all a lot of noise. I could tell that neither dog was in trouble. When they separated, both dogs had a small nick, but otherwise they were fine. From that day, Bea only has to look at Amber, and she knows to step down.

"Amber took to Agility in record time – the only trouble is keeping up with her! She goes like a rocket, and it feels as if she's two miles in front. But when we get it right, she's amazing. The first clear round we ever got was competing against 260 dogs, mostly Border Collies, and she came first. I now have a cabinet full of trophies, and Amber is still only two-and-a-half years old.

"She is a dog who can never get enough. We go to Agility classes four times a week, Obedience once a week, and she's still got tons of energy. Her idea is to go home and then wind up the other dogs and get them to play. She's a cracking dog, and I wouldn't want her any other way.

LAID-BACK DOUGAL

"Dougal, a Collie/Retriever cross, was the next to join our pack. He was adopted by my partner, Chris, as a one-year-old, and then came to live with us.

"He has more of the Retriever in him than the Collie, in the sense that he is far more laid-back. He loves people, and loves his Agility, but he never gets hyped up. He is happy to come home

Dougal: He loves to work, but he is also happy to take life easy.

from training or a show and have a sleep on his bed, whereas Amber has only just got going.

"Dougal had some basic obedience training when he was adopted, and he has never given us a day's trouble. In many ways, he is a dream dog to have from a rehoming centre because he is so easy.

"He's more sensitive than the other dogs. He doesn't like the cold, and, being mostly black, he can't tolerate the heat. We have actually pulled him out of a couple of competitions because he could not stand the heat, whereas our other Agility dogs wouldn't even notice.

"I have learnt how to use a stripping knife, and if it is really hot, I take out his undercoat. He is as good as gold. He looks at me as if he is saying: 'Thank goodness you're getting rid of all that fur.'

MURPHY'S LAW

"Murphy is supposed to be a Collie, but he just keeps on growing. He looked like a Collie when I saw him at around four months, but his legs have just got longer and longer. He is now a year old, and Amber and Jake can walk underneath him without ducking! He really is a gentle giant.

"Right from the start, Murphy was so easy to train. He is awesomely intelligent. You see him sitting with his head on one side, and he is obviously thinking. Then he trots off, and gets into a cupboard or something. You can see that he's been working it all out in his head.

"He's fanatical about Flyball. We used to take him to watch training sessions when he was a puppy, and he was always straining to have a go. The first time we tried him on the Flyball box,

Murphy: The gentle giant that keeps on growing!

he picked it up after two or three hits. Now we have to be careful when we watch Flyball videos at home, because Murphy tries to get the ball from the TV!

FIVE IS THE LIMIT?

"I have been amazingly lucky with all the dogs I have rehomed, and after getting Bea, I have never considered any other route. Dogs Trust gives you help and support if you need it, and so you do not feel as if you are on your own.

"I have always said that five dogs is my limit – but sometimes I am very tempted. The rehoming centre at Evesham rings me up if they have a Collie cross that needs a home, and I can often help because I know so many people through Agility and Flyball. The trouble is, when I go to see the dog, I find myself thinking: 'That's such a cracking dog – maybe I could go up to six!'"

CHAPTER SEVEN

SOCIALISATION

Socialisation is the process of educating a dog about the world he lives in. A dog needs to encounter everyday sights and sounds so that he learns to be confident and is able to take all situations in his stride.

If you are adopting a puppy, you have a relatively easy task ahead. A pup absorbs new experiences like a sponge, and the more situations he encounters, the more adaptable and well-rounded an individual he will become. The critical period for socialisation is between 50-84 days when a pup is highly impressionable to all new learning experiences. During this period, spend as much time as you can with your pup, as it will enhance the bonding process, and he will start to look on you as his leader.

An adult dog who has been poorly socialised will need time and patience. He has a lot of ground to make up, and he may be fearful about strange sights and sounds. This is often the case with ex-racing Greyhounds, whose horizons have been limited to the kennel they live in and the track where they race.

However, it is essential to work at socialising an adult, otherwise the dog will become increasingly apprehensive. It is no fun for the dog to be frightened every times he steps out of the house, and you will be increasingly limited as to where you can go because you will be worried about your dog's reaction.

AT HOME

Most dogs are quick to find their feet, and it should not be long before a puppy or an adult is able to relax in his home surroundings. You may find that there is the odd surprise, such as when the dog first encounters the vacuum cleaner, or when he hears the sound of the washing machine. If your dog seems particularly worried, rather than just showing initial concern, try the following:

• Show the dog you have a treat, and encourage him to approach the vacuum cleaner, for example, which should be switched off.

• Do not force the dog to come closer than he

If you have never seen a vacuum cleaner before, it can seem like a scary monster!

ready to play with if this works better for your dog), and when you switch on the machine, walk away from it and call your dog to you. Let the dog get used to the noise while you are distracting him with treats or a game.

- When you feel the dog is starting to relax, switch off the machine.
- You will have to work at familiarising your dog with the vacuum cleaner over a number of sessions, but if you persevere, he will learn he has nothing to fear.

NOTE: This training exercise can be adapted so that you can help your dog to become accustomed to all household machines, and anything else he is concerned about.

SPOOKY SITUATIONS

If a dog has been poorly socialised, he will often 'spook' at strange sights and sounds, which he sees as potential threats. For example, someone holding an umbrella or wearing a crash helmet could provoke your dog to bark or shy away. It is simply because the dog has never been exposed to such a situation, and he does not know how to react.

For puppies who have not encountered the outside world, and for poorly socialised dogs, you can manufacture situations so that the dog learns that he can cope with the unexpected.

Set up the following scenarios at home:

- Leave an umbrella open on the ground, so your dog can investigate. Give the dog lots of verbal encouragement, keeping your voice up-beat and matter-of-fact. This will help the dog to realise there is nothing to fear.

wants. Simply call him to you, and reward him, without making a big deal of it.

- If your dog is especially nervous, leave it there, and end the training session on a positive note.
- Next time you get the vacuum cleaner out, encourage the dog to come a little closer. Let him sniff the machine so that he can work out that it is not a scary monster. Give lots of praise, and reward him.
- Now try moving the vacuum cleaner. Your dog may start back, but keep moving the machine, and hold out a treat for him. Be patient, and your dog will make up his mind to be brave.
- The first time you switch on the vacuum cleaner, make sure the door is closed so that the dog does not run off in fright. It is far better to help him overcome his fears rather than letting him run away.
- Arm yourself with lots of treats (or have a toy

- Try opening and shutting the umbrella, acting as though you are playing a game. When the dog approaches, reward him with a treat.
- Then, put the dog on a lead, and walk for a few paces, carrying the umbrella. Praise and reward the dog when he walks calmly at your side.

TAKE YOUR TIME

If you have a nervous dog, you may have to work at this scenario (and those listed below) over a number of sessions. Remember, it is always better to progress slowly rather than overwhelming your dog, which will increase his anxiety levels.

- Recruit friends or family to appear wearing sunglasses, a hat, or a crash helmet. Each person should have a treat, so the dog is encouraged to approach, and is then rewarded.
- Bang two saucepan lids together. Your dog may start at the unexpected noise, but then encourage him to approach you and give him a treat. Try this a few times until the dog ceases to react to the sound.
- You can get a CD with a soundtrack that includes, traffic, trains, bells chiming, and aeroplanes taking off. If you have a nervous dog, put this on at home (initially so that it is barely audible) where the dog feels relaxed. The dog will soak up these sounds unconsciously, and will have less to fear when he goes outside and has to cope with real-life situations.

A young dog will soak up new experiences like a sponge.

OUTSIDE THE HOME

If you have adopted a puppy, you will have to be careful about venturing into the outside world until he has completed his vaccinations (see Chapter Nine). However, this does not mean that your pup has to be confined to the house and garden until he is fully protected.

- Take your puppy to visit friends who have a dog, as long as you know the dog is healthy.
- Take your puppy out for short trips in the car (see page 98).
- Park in a shopping centre, and carry the pup to the nearest bench. If you sit there for a while, the pup can become accustomed to all the different sights and sounds. Few people can resist a pup, so he will also benefit from getting lots of attention.
- Many veterinary practices run puppy socialisation classes. They are generally open to pups after they have received their first vaccination.

*S*haron and Joe Beer both grew up with dogs, and they decided that a Greyhound would fit in with their lifestyle. First, Dylan arrived, followed a year later by Poppy – and they are perfectly happy to share their home with two cats.

"When Dylan first arrived, he was really, really nervous," said Sharon. "He had been tried as a racing dog, but he didn't chase, so he was put up for rehoming. He was tested with cats, and because he was a non-chaser, we were pretty confident that he would be okay.

"In fact, when Dylan first came into the house, he was attacked by the cat. We didn't know it at the time, but she was pregnant, and she took exception to having her territory invaded. Poor Dylan was so frightened, he ran away.

BUILDING TRUST

"On the first day, Dylan cowered behind the sofa and wouldn't come out. We tried to get him to have a drink of water, but he refused to move. He wouldn't even come out for food. We let him stay where he was, and the next morning when Joe came into the sitting room, he tried to bolt straight through the window.

"It took weeks before he would trust us. We decided not to make a big issue of his nervousness. We tried not to pester him or overwhelm him – we just let him do things in his own time.

"He was worried by men – particularly if they wore dark clothes – but lots of things frightened him, both at home and when we went out. There was one time when I put up an umbrella, and he slipped his collar and ran away. I don't

think he was cruelly treated, but I don't think he was treated with much gentleness. It was obvious that he hadn't been socialised at all – everything worried him.

"Over the first year, he learned to trust us and he became increasingly relaxed – he even gave up worrying about the cat. But the big change came when Poppy arrived.

GROWING CONFIDENCE

"We adopted her from the Dogs Trust rehoming centre at Ilfracombe, and they advised us to choose a female. From the day she arrived, the two Greyhounds got on amazingly well, and having her around has given Dylan so much confidence. It was as if Poppy was teaching Dylan how to behave like a dog. He had no idea how to play with toys or what to do with a chew until he watched her.

Dylan: He needed time to overcome his nervousness.

Poppy: Her top priority is food.

RELAXING

"We live near the beach, and both the Greyhounds are fine off the lead. They chase after other dogs – big and small – but it's just a game.

"Dylan loves to copy other dogs. The other day, he saw a dog running round and barking, and he suddenly did the same – although he never normally barks. He looked at me as if to say: 'Look at me barking!'

"There have been some difficult times – Poppy didn't have a clue about housetraining, and that took some time to sort out – but now both dogs have settled well.

"Greyhounds are the most wonderful companions. They are so calm and gentle – I find it relaxing just to be with them."

"At the same time that we adopted Poppy, we acquired a kitten. Poppy had been tested safe with cats, so we thought she would be okay. In fact, having a small, furry creature running about was quite a test for her. Dylan wasn't interested, but Poppy would prick her ears and look very keen. I just used my voice to tell her "No" every time she looked at the kitten, or the cat, and she realised that they were not for chasing.

"Poppy was a real nutter when we got her, and although she's settled down, she's still quite a handful. Her top priority is food – and she doesn't mind how she gets hold of it. She's a terrible bin raider, and nothing is safe if it is left on a counter. She's taken care of a joint of beef that was defrosting, and she even ate a packet of sugar when I left it out after making a cup of tea!

Dylan is now brave enough to share a sofa with the cat.

CAR TRAVEL

A dog must learn to settle quietly in the car – for his safety, and for the safety of the driver and passengers. The best plan is to confine the dog to a specific area of the car (see page 34 for information on car travel equipment).

You may have a dog that is used to travelling in a car. For example, ex-racing Greyhounds, who are poorly socialised in many ways, are often excellent travellers, as they are used to being transported to and from the track. In fact, nearly all dogs adapt swiftly to car travel, and most learn to love trips out in the car.

If your dog is unsettled in the car, try the following:

- Start by putting your dog in the car and allowing him to settle before you switch on the engine. Then leave the engine on for a few minutes before setting off.

- To begin with, go for short trips that end somewhere nice (such as the park). In this way, the dog will learn to associate the car with something pleasurable.
- If the dog barks or whines, do not shout at him to be quiet. This will only encourage him to make more noise (see page 114). Ignore him, and try switching on the radio. This will help to drown his protests, and he may find it soothing.
- If the dog has a tendency to be car-sick, do not feed him before you go out. Most dogs cease being car-sick once they have got used to the motion of the car. If the problem persists, consult your vet.
- When you arrive at your destination, teach the dog to "Wait". Then attach his lead, and tell him to "Come" when you are ready. A dog that tries to leap from the car the moment the door is opened is a danger to himself and to others.

BROADENING HORIZONS

Once your dog has had a chance to settle in his new home (or when your pup has completed his vaccinations), you will be ready to begin socialisation in earnest. It will make matters a great deal easier if your dog is walking reasonably well on the lead. If you have problems in this area, you will need to do some work at home in the garden before going out in public (see page 79).

The best plan is to find a location that is relatively quiet, like a residential area, so you can

Teach your dog to "wait" before he jumps out of the car.

test your dog's reactions without overwhelming him. For these first outings, make sure you are not trying to do the shopping or look after children at the same time. You will need to concentrate on the dog.

- Walk along with the dog at your side, giving him lots of verbal encouragement.
- With any luck, the dog will stride out, taking an interest in his surroundings but not showing undue concern.
- The traffic will not be constant, but you will be able to judge your dog's reaction to it. The majority of dogs will not be affected by the noise, but some are more sound-sensitive than others. If your dog shies away from a car, or is clearly unhappy, you will need to confine your walks to quiet areas to begin with. As the dog grows in confidence, you can try more challenging environments.

In a busier location, such as a shopping centre, you may encounter situations that your dog has not experienced before. You will be walking among more people: some with bags, some with pushchairs, and some with shopping trolleys. You may come across a lorry being unloaded, a queue of people waiting for the bus, or some road-works. If your dog shows concern, do not force him to walk past. Try the following:

- Stop for a few moments so that the dog has a chance to look and absorb what is going on.
- Then encourage the dog to continue. You can use a treat, but only give it when the dog is moving – otherwise you are rewarding him for standing still.

Start off in a quiet location so that the dog is relaxed and confident.

- Make your tone brisk and businesslike. Do not sympathise with the dog, or he will think that there is a genuine cause for concern.
- Do not make the mistake of avoiding whatever has scared your dog. Continue with your walk, and then return to the spot where the dog showed concern.
- It may be that whatever scared your dog is no longer there – in which case, you can carry on with your walk, and the dog will not build up a bad association with the place.
- If the problem (for example, road-works) is around, repeat the exercise outlined above.

Gradually progress to a more challenging environment.

Let the dog look, and reward him for moving on.

If you have a nervous dog, it may take some time to overcome fears, but the more the dog is exposed to different situations, the more confident he will become. The dog will learn that nothing nasty happens to him when he encounters new sights and sounds, and he will gradually become accustomed to more challenging environments.

FINDING A MENTOR

Dogs can gain confidence from each other; if you have a nervous dog, try to find someone who has a dog of sound temperament who can come on walks with you. When your dog sees the other dog walking past potentially spooky situations without a care in the world, it will give him the courage to follow suit.

SOCIALISING SITUATIONS

Be inventive about creating opportunities where you can socialise your dog. In most cases, you can fit this into your regular routine, but sometimes you may need to go further afield. Although this may seem like hard work, it will pay off as your dog becomes increasingly adaptable in his outlook.

- Go to the local park where you will meet other people out walking, as well as giving your dog a chance to play with other dogs. Arrange to meet up with a friend who has a dog that is well trained and sound in temperament. This will provide a safe, sensible playmate for your dog. When the play session is over, your friend can recall her dog and attach his lead. Your dog will see that the fun is over, and this will mean he is more likely to respond to you (see Recall, page 83).
- While you are in the park, go to the children's play area (you will probably have to stay outside the immediate area) and let your dog watch children at play.
- There may be a game of football taking place in the park. Stop for a few minutes, and let the dog take in the situation (see Chasing page 114).
- A railway station will provide lots of socialising opportunities: stairs, tunnels, bridges, as well as trains. If your dog is concerned, distract his attention with treats (see above). You can also arrange to meet a friend who has a dog at the station. Your dog will be so interested in meeting his new friend, he will ignore the surroundings.

- A shopping mall will give your dog experience of walking through crowds. You may also come across revolving doors and escalators.
- A walk around a supermarket car park can be very educational. The dog will see lots of people pushing trolleys, lorries unloading, and cars driving in and out. You may find a recycling centre, and your dog can get used to the bangs and crashes as people recycle their waste.
- If you do not have children, take a walk past the local primary school when the children are arriving, or when they are going home. The dog will get lots of attention, and he will meet children of all ages.
- If you live in a town, you will need to give your dog an opportunity to meet livestock, such as sheep, cattle, horses and poultry. A trip to a country fair provides an ideal opportunity to meet livestock in a controlled situation. If your dog shows an undue interest, work at distracting his attention with a treat. You can use exactly the same method used for introducing dogs to small animals (see page 52). Remember to reward the dog every time he looks away from the animals.

Obviously, you need to keep the dog on a lead when you are around livestock, but it is still important that he learns acceptable behaviour. If your dog is very focused on the animals, you will need to keep repeating the experience until he responds to you.

You may need to take a trip out of town to complete your dog's education.

THE ADAPTABLE DOG

Socialisation does not have to be hard work. It gives you the opportunity to go out and about with your dog, and this will help to build up a good relationship. The aim of every owner is to have a dog that is a pleasure to own; if you give your dog a chance to learn about the world around him, you will go a long way towards achieving your goal.

CHAPTER EIGHT

TROUBLE-SHOOTING

Despite all your hard work, there are times when you can get stuck when you are training your dog. This may be a problem with teaching a particular training exercise, or it may be a behavioural problem that you are struggling to overcome.

There are a number of reasons why training problems can occur:

- You are not making your meaning clear, so the dog is confused.
- You may not have trained your dog with positive rewards to encourage him to do what you ask him.
- The dog may be nervous and is 'misbehaving' through fear or anxiety.
- The dog may have learnt a bad habit in his previous home, and so he needs a retraining programme to break the cycle.

If you hit a problem, do not despair! If you employ positive, reward-based training methods, you will nearly always succeed. Teach your dog

that it is more rewarding to do as you ask rather than follow his own agenda, and he will come round to your way of thinking.

To tackle a training or behavioural problem, you need to take a step back and examine what is going on. Try to see the situation from your dog's perspective, and then think what might help him to move on.

If you need expert help from an experienced trainer or be behaviourist, do not see it as an admission of failure. It is far better to take positive steps to overcome a problem rather than struggling on your own.

PICKING UP CLUES

In order to understand what is going on in your dog's mind, you need to be able to read his body language. This will provide the strongest clues if you know what to look for. It also puts you in a better position because you will be able to anticipate his reactions and his likely behaviour.

- A positive body posture and wagging tail

READING THE SIGNS

A relaxed, happy dog, with an upright stance and wagging tail.

A nervous type, who wants to appear submissive.

Aggressive or fearful? This type of behaviour can be prompted by both emotions.

Happy to play? The black dog has no reservations, the yellow Labrador is not quite so sure.

Spoiling for a fight: This dog is even more assertive because he is on the lead.

indicates happiness and confidence.

- A crouched body posture with ears back and tail down will often be adopted by a dog who is being told off. He is downcast and submissive.
- A timid dog will try to make himself as small as possible, lowering his bodyline, keeping his tail between his legs and his ears well back.
- A bold dog will look strong and alert. His ears will be pricked or forward, and his tail will be held high.
- A dog who raises his hackles (lifting the fur along his topline) is making himself look big and scary. This may be a prelude to aggressive behaviour, but in many more cases, it is a sign of apprehension. The dog is anxious and unsure about how he should cope with the situation.
- An assertive dog will meet other dogs with a hard, open stare. If the dog is challenged, he will growl, bare his teeth, and the corners of his mouth will be drawn forward. His ears will be erect and he will appear tense in every muscle.
- A nervous dog may often show aggressive behaviour as a means of self-protection rather than assertion (see page 110). If threatened, this dog will lower his head and flatten his ears. The corners of his mouth may be drawn back, and he may bark or whine.

    Do not confuse the 'smiling' dog with an aggressive dog. Some dogs will curl up their top lip and show their teeth when they are greeting people. Generally, the body posture is low and the tail is wagging. This is an act of submission, and would be used to greet higher-ranking animals in the pack.

CONFUSING THE ISSUE

While you are reading your dog's body language, he is looking at you to try to understand what you want, and how he should react. He is also listening to your voice to pick up commands, and to find out if you are pleased or angry with him.

It is very easy to confuse a dog by sending out mixed messages, so before you start working on the dog, check out the following:

- Are you making yourself exciting to your dog with positive body language? See page 70.
- Are you adopting a positive, encouraging tone of voice? See page 71.
- Are your commands easy to understand? See page 69-72.
- Are you rewarding correct behaviour at the moment it is offered? See page 71.
- Are you proving a suitable reward that will motivate your dog so that he wants to do as you ask? See page 72.

ASSERTIVE DOGS

There are some dogs in rehoming centres who have received little in the way of training in their previous home, and they have got into the way of doing exactly as they please. Male dogs are more likely to be assertive, but this is not always the case. Any dog who has tested the boundaries may start to fancy his chances. An assertive dog may show any (or all) of the following:

- Poor response to general training exercises.
- Easily distracted in more challenging environments, such as in the park.

- A tendency to break house rules, e.g. getting on the furniture.
- Possessive over toys or food, and sometimes guarding his own space, e.g. his bed.
- Aggressive towards other dogs, or towards people (see pages 110-112)

YOUR RESPONSE

Your task is to train your dog using positive rewards so that he wants to respond to you rather than pleasing himself, and he understands the boundaries you have set for him. Try the following:

- Make training fun. Work at simple exercises, which give you the opportunity to praise and reward your dog.
- Restrict his access to toys, and only bring out a toy for special, fun sessions, which your dog will find especially rewarding.
- Allocate a few minutes every day to grooming, regardless of whether the dog needs it or not. This helps to establish a bond between you, and the dog also learns to accept all-over handling.

Use every opportunity to show the dog you are in control.

- When you are leaving the house, put the dog on his lead, and make sure he waits until you go through the door first. Then reward him with a treat. This is an important safety measure, and it shows the dog that you are in control. It also applies when you take the dog in the car. Tell him to "Wait" before he jumps out, and then reward him for co-operating.
- If the dog is on the sofa, or seems put out when you approach his bed, produce his favourite toy or a really tasty treat, and encourage him to come to you. You have avoided a confrontation, and the dog has chosen to abandon his position in preference of doing as you ask.
- When the dog is feeding, drop some treats into his bowl. Rather than growling at you for going near his food, he will welcome the interference.
- Provide mental stimulation so that your dog has a chance to use his brain in a positive way. This can be as simple as teaching a few tricks, or you may decide to get involved with one of the specialist canine activities (see page 86).

ANXIOUS DOGS

Some dogs are born worriers, while others become anxious because of what has happened to them. At a rehoming centre, you will see some dogs who are more nervous than others, and they often need special help to boost their confidence. In some cases, a dog may have been poorly socialised (see Chapter Seven). This can sometimes be the case with ex-racing Greyhounds. With patience, these dogs will learn to adapt, as long as you progress slowly and with sensitivity.

There are some dogs who become so anxious when they are left alone that they develop specific behavioural traits. This could include:

- Destructive behaviour
- Soiling the house
- Constant attention-seeking
- Excessive barking when left alone.

A dog who is showing any of these behavioural traits is telling you that he cannot cope on his own. He has lost confidence, and his inappropriate behaviour is the only way he can express his anxiety. Although the type of behaviour the dog is showing may appear fairly daunting, it can be dramatically improved with time and patience.

YOUR RESPONSE

- In the initial stages of training, you may find a stair-gate is a useful aid. You can use it between doorways so the dog can still see and hear you, even though he is not in the same room. This will start to build up his confidence, so that he does not feel deserted when you are not close at hand.
- It may be worth investing in an indoor crate. The dog will learn to feel safe and secure in his 'den', and it obviously eliminates the problems of destructiveness and soiling. However, an indoor crate should only be used for limited periods.
- A boredom-busting toy, filled with treats, will keep your dog occupied so he is less likely to fret when he is left on his own.
- Do not make a big fuss when you leave your dog – or when you return. If you are calm

An artificial barrier can be used so that the dog can still hear and see you, but he is also learning that he can cope on his own.

and matter-of-fact, the dog will not see your comings and goings as such a big deal.
- When you return, give it 10 minutes before you go to the dog. Again, this takes the tension out of the situation.
- Try a few mock departures, putting on your coat, or jangling your keys, and then returning after a short interval. This should prevent him from developing negative associations with the signs of your departure, and getting worked up in anticipation of being separated from you.

Be patient with your dog, and use all opportunities to praise and reward him for good behaviour. Work at a few basic exercises, or teach him fun tricks, and this will help to boost his self-esteem. In time, the dog will realise that separation is only temporary, and he will feel able to cope on his own without resorting to undesirable behaviour.

There are now drugs available through your veterinary surgeon to help you with the training process. They will help to reduce your dog's anxiety levels, and therefore make him more responsive to training programmes, but they will not replace training.

Diane Clark adopted her first dog, Tiger-Chi, a white smooth-haired Chihuahua, two years ago. Now she has three Chihuahuas, who pretty much rule the roost!

"It all started when I went shopping with my daughter, Shauna, who works for Dogs Trust. We went to a pet shop to buy a bed for my Whippet, Jumble, and I came across a beautiful carrying case. I said to Shauna: 'I've found the bag – all I need is the dog to put in it.'

"Jumble was 14 at the time, and soon afterwards he became ill. One day, Shauna gave me a ring from the rehoming centre at Evesham, saying, 'You've got to come and see this one.' There I met Tiger-Chi. He was two years old.

"When he first came home, he knew nothing.

I had to train him from scratch, and he didn't trust me. I think he must have suffered some cruelty because, to begin with, if I tried to pick him up, he would curl himself up into a tiny ball. I took him to the training class at the rehoming centre, and he learned things very quickly. He now does mini Agility, and the staff at the centre are really proud of him.

"Tiger got on with Jumble right from the start, and I honestly believe that he gave Jumble another six months of life. When Jumble died, Tiger became depressed, so I was desperate to get another Chihuahua. I contacted all the rehoming charities, but there was nothing available. In the end, I decided to buy a puppy.

"Rio is a red, smooth-coated Chihuahua, and he is now 12 months old. He's a little devil – full of

Tiger-Chi: He gave Jumble another six months of life.

Tiger and Rio (front) got on well with each other from the start.

mischief, but adorable. He gets on fine with Tiger, and he loves my granddaughter. She is 11 months old, and he likes to stand guard by her pram.

"The third Chihuahua to join us was Jorge, a beautiful long-coated red dog. He was found wandering with his sister, who had broken her leg. The veterinary nurse who first looked after them adopted the sister, and I adopted Jorge. They reckoned he was seven years old, but he is so lively, I think he must be younger. He's a lovely, laid-back dog. My guess is that he had an elderly owner. He was quite well trained when he arrived, so he must have been well looked after at one time.

"I took Tiger and Rio to meet Jorge at the rehoming centre, and they all seemed to get on with each other. But when I brought Jorge home, the trouble started. Tiger went for Jorge, and even though Jorge has been with us a year, I still don't trust them together. Tiger is a very loving, affectionate dog, but he is very jealous. He doesn't like me paying attention to Jorge.

"I have been given a lot of help by the training and behaviour advisor at Evesham, and the situation is beginning to improve. I keep each of the dogs in indoor crates during the night, but in the morning, I let them outside together. I have now got to the stage where I can sit on the sofa with Jorge on my left, with Rio on the back of the sofa at my neck, and with Tiger on my right. He does growl a bit, but he is learning to put up with it. I think the secret is for me to be less tense, and then they will start to relax.

"Despite the problems, I wouldn't swap any of my dogs. I know I spoil them – each dog has his own jacket, his own silver collar, and his own cushion – and they have a huge toy box. They mean everything to me – my dogs are my life."

Collecting Jorge from the rehoming centre.

When you are ready, arrange to meet a dog of impeccable character, so that your dog learns he does not need to come out with all guns blazing every time he sees another dog.

AGGRESSIVE DOGS

Most aggression is caused by competition for resources. The causes may be territorial, food, or even a favourite toy. But aggression towards other dogs can often be attributed to fear. The dog is worried about meeting other dogs, and decides the best policy is to get in first. This type of dog may have been poorly socialised, and has not had the chance to interact with other dogs and learn canine manners. It is helpful to learn as much as you can about your dog's body language (see page 103), so that you can interpret his reaction.

At Dogs Trust rehoming centres, every dog that is put up for rehoming is tested with another dog and the reaction is evaluated. Great care is taken to ensure that dogs with aggressive tendencies are not rehomed with families that already have a dog. As long as introductions are supervised (see page 49), most dogs will learn to live in peace with each other.

If your dog is wary of other dogs, there are a number of points to bear in mind:

- If your dog shows any sign of aggression towards another dog, do not stroke him, pick him up, or reassure him. As far as the dog is concerned, you are endorsing his behaviour.
- Avoid tension on the lead, as this can make a dog feel bolder than he is, as he is looking on you as back-up.
- If you meet another dog, allow the two dogs to sniff each other, and then call your dog to come away with you. Make sure you have a really tasty treat as a reward.
- Avoid confrontations with dogs that you know are aggressive. It is much easier to cross the road, or give the dog a wide berth, rather than inviting trouble.
- Arrange to meet up with a friend that has a dog of impeccable temperament. A dog who has perfect canine manners will teach your dog that he has nothing to fear, and he will start to learn the correct responses.
- If you go to a training class, make sure the instructor is experienced in socialising dogs. Do not allow yourself to be put in a corner with your dog, as this will exacerbate the situation.
- If you are worried about your dog's reaction, fit him with a muzzle. If you know your dog cannot do any harm, you will be more relaxed, which will transmit to the dog and calm him.

WATCH WORD

A useful tip is to train your dog to respond to the "Watch" command. If the dog turns to look at you when you command "Watch", you have a means of diverting his attention and focusing it on you. This can be used when you want to stop your dog eyeing another dog. It can also be used on dogs that have a tendency to chase, giving you the means of refocusing the dog's attention away from the object of his desires, whether it is livestock, a jogger, or a bicycle (see page 114).

- Start with the dog at your side, and show him a treat. If you have a toy-mad dog, use his favourite toy.
- Give the command "Watch", and as the dog looks towards the treat/toy, praise him. Reward him with the treat or a game with the toy.
- Build this exercise up in easy stages, gradually increasing the amount of time the dog has to wait for his reward after you have given the "Watch" command.
- Do not over-use this command or the dog will become bored and disinterested. Keep it for when you need it, and then you can be confident of a good response. Make sure you reward the dog with his favourite treats, or give him an extra-special play session with his toy.

PEOPLE AGGRESSION

Unfortunately, there are dogs who have suffered such terrible problems that they have resorted to being aggressive with people. This is a complete breakdown of the man-dog relationship, where the dog has lost all trust in people. This is a major problem to deal with, and dogs with a known history of people aggression will not be put up for adoption. At Dogs Trust, the following steps may be taken:

- Training and behaviour experts will assess a dog with aggressive tendencies, and will work on a programme of rehabilitation. If this proves successful, the dog may be adopted, but only with the proviso that the new owners are highly experienced and will continue to work with behaviour experts.

Teach your dog to "Watch" so that he learns to focus his attention on you.

• There are some dogs who are never going to be happy living with people. Dogs Trust has a Sanctuary, which is suitable for dogs that are safe to socialise with other dogs, but are unsuitable for rehoming. Here, dogs can live in a stress-free environment, and this eliminates their need to behave aggressively.

If your dog suddenly becomes aggressive, do not delay in seeking professional advice. This is not a problem you should try to solve on your own. First get the dog checked over by a vet to see if there is a physical reason, such as pain, to account for your dog's change in behaviour. If there is no medical cause, your vet should refer you to an experienced behaviourist who can help you to find out what has triggered the change in the dog's behaviour, and can plan a retraining programme.

JUMPING UP

No one likes a dog that keeps jumping up, and it can be positively dangerous if you have small children or elderly people who come to visit.

If you have a puppy, it is important to nip this behaviour in the bud before it becomes a problem, but you may have an older dog who has got into the habit of jumping up in order to get attention.

This is an area of training where you need to

Jumping up is an attention-seeking device. If you ignore the dog until all four feet are on the ground, he will soon learn that jumping up does not get him anywhere.

be 100 per cent consistent. You cannot make a fuss of your dog because he has jumped up to give you a lovely greeting, and then tell him off the next day because he has done the same thing – but this time with muddy paws. Your dog will have no idea why he is being praised one moment and reprimanded the next. He will get mixed messages, and will begin to lose his positive relationship with you.

To stop your dog jumping up, try the following:

- When the dog jumps up, turn away from him, avoiding eye contact. You can use a command, such as "Off".
- Do not touch the dog or attempt to push him off. The dog will see this as a positive response. Make your body language as negative as possible, turning your back to the dog. If the dog is not getting any attention, he will see there is no point being on his hind feet.
- The moment the dog goes back on all four feet, give lots of praise, and reward him with a treat.
- If he tries to jump up again, repeat the exercise. In time, your dog will realise that, when he jumps up, he is ignored, but when all four feet are on the ground, he gets the attention he craves and is also rewarded with a treat.

MEETING VISITORS

There are some dogs who are fine with the family but they jump up and get over-excited when visitors arrive. An excitable dog is likely to become hyped up, and a nervous dog may shrink away or bark excessively (see page 114).

Arrange for visitors to come, and turn it into a training session so that your dog learns to react calmly.

With both scenarios, the dog is expressing his insecurity. He has started to look on the house as his territory where he feels safe, and now strangers are invading his space.

Very often, a dog who feels insecure is only too happy if you show him how to behave rather than letting him decide for himself. Start by inviting some doggie friends to the house and set up a training situation.

- As soon as the doorbell rings, put your dog on the lead and take him to the sitting room.
- Ask someone else to open the door. It eases the tension if the dog is not at the door as people come in.
- As the visitors come in, provide each of them with a treat. Then take your dog to greet each visitor in turn, and let him Sit for a treat. Encourage the visitors to be calm and low-key

in their body language, so that the dog does not get over-excited or feel threatened.

- Keep the lead slack so that the dog does not feel any tension. If he tries to jump up, give a command, such as "Off", and ask the dog to "Sit". Make sure he is only given his reward when he has all four feet on the ground.
- After the initial greeting, keep the dog on the lead while the visitors take their seats. Put the dog in the "Down" position by your side; if no one pays him any attention, he will relax.
- If your dog appears to be calm and settled, you can let him off-lead after half an hour or so, and he can go and see the visitors on his own terms.
- If the dog still appears tense, it is better to keep him on-lead while visitors are around. When he becomes used to the situation, you can progress to letting him off-lead.

EXCESSIVE BARKING

A dog may bark excessively in the following situations:

- When visitors come to the house (see above).
- When the dog is left on his own (see page 106).
- When the dog is in the car (see page 98).

In most cases, excessive barking is the expression of a hyped-up dog. The dog feels insecure, and he is giving voice to his feelings. In some cases, the dog may be barking to keep strangers away from his territory, which may be the house or the car.

In all these situations, you need to ignore the behaviour you don't like (i.e. barking), and reward the behaviour you like (i.e. being quiet).

You may think that you are not doing anything when you ignore your dog, but do not underestimate how powerful a weapon this is when a dog wants attention.

CHASING

There are some breeds that have a strong instinct to chase, and although all types of dog may exhibit some form of this behaviour, it is the Collie types who can become obsessive.

If you do not want an instinct to develop, the best plan is never to awaken it. If a Collie puppy spends all his time chasing balls, his instinct to chase will thrive. If you do not play these sort of games, the pup will still show some degree of instinctive behaviour, but it is less likely to become an overwhelming passion.

If you take on an adult rescued dog who has a tendency to chase, you can retrain using the following methods:

- Get your dog fixated on a toy (this shouldn't be difficult), and bring it out only when you are working at refocusing his attention. This

Some dogs have a strong desire to chase, and they must learn to turn away from temptation – prompted by an extra-special reward

will give the toy rarity value, so that your dog is desperate to play with it.

- Find a potential 'chase' situation, such as standing on the touch-line while a football match is in progress. When the dog fixes his eye on the ball, attract his attention with the toy.
- When the dog responds, step a few paces back, and have a really good game. The dog must feel that the reward of playing with his toy is even greater than eyeing the ball.
- Work at this over a period of time. It will help if you introduce the "Watch" command (see page 111) so that the dog knows he must turn away from what he is looking at and refocus on you.
- Work at all basic training exercises to improve your control and to get the dog used to listening to you (see Chapter Six).
- Think about getting involved with a specialist canine activity, such as Competitive Obedience or Agility (see page 86). This gives a focus to his mental energy, and he will not be so inclined to find his own entertainment.

SUMMING UP

Training a dog is always a challenge, but it can be a very rewarding experience. It is important to be patient with your dog, particularly in the settling-in period when he is getting to know his new home and family. Remember, Rome was not built in a day, and it may take some time before your dog fits in with your lifestyle. Bear the following points in mind:

- The more time you spend with your dog, the better. The dog will bond with you, and will want to please you.

Training can sometimes be tough, but if you work through the problems, the rewards are incomparable.

- Allocate a time every day to training. This does not need to be lengthy – five minutes will do – but it provides a regular opportunity to reinforce the messages you want to put over, and to reward the dog for co-operating.
- Be consistent in your training so your dog does not become confused.
- Be generous with your rewards: verbal praise, and stroking should be combined with food treats or a game with a toy.
- If you are asking your dog to do something really difficult, such as focusing on you rather than another dog, make sure the reward is worth getting. Select his favourite treat (see page 72), or bring out the toy you reserve for training (see page 72).
- End training sessions on a positive note, with an exercise you know your dog can do. This will make him feel successful, and you can reward him with a treat or a game. The dog will view training as a positive experience, and he will be keen to work the next time you ask.

CHAPTER NINE

HEALTH CARE

Rescued dogs are really no different to any other dog except that they come in all shapes and sizes, and, unlike the pedigree dog, we have no idea who their grandparents are – and sometimes not even their parents!

Because most rescued dogs are cross-breeds, there is some evidence that they are less likely to suffer from hereditary diseases and therefore, perhaps, they may be a little more healthy. However, these dogs have been living in an environment where they are close to many other dogs, so they may have a higher than average chance of picking up some of the kennel environment diseases such as Kennel Cough. But essentially their health care is exactly the same as for any other dog.

Most rescue kennels have a very responsible attitude to the health care of the dogs in their rehoming centres, but it is well worth asking the centre a little bit about what veterinary attention the dogs have had. The better rescue organisations will have vaccinated their dogs

and treated them for worms and fleas. For puppies, the importance of correct treatment is even greater.

Where drugs are mentioned in this section the generic name of the drug is used rather than the trade name. Some are prescription-only medicines (POM), and so may only be obtained from your veterinary surgeon. Some others are available in pet shops, and careful study of packaging will reveal the generic name.

VACCINATION

Modern vaccines have gone a long way towards eliminating some of the worst canine diseases: Distemper is now relatively uncommon, whereas 30 years ago it was the scourge of some cities, and the dreadful emergence of Canine Parvovirus in the late 70s has now reduced to a trickle. But we should not be complacent as there are still outbreaks of disease, and vaccination still plays a major part in disease control.

Because rehoming centres take dogs from a wide variety of places varying from private

At rehoming centres, puppies may receive an initial vaccination as they are in a vulnerable situation.

homes to ex-strays from local authorities, it is easy for disease to be imported. It is therefore not uncommon to find a sporadic incidence of disease problems and good rehoming centres use vaccination to help in their control. Of course, disease incidence varies from one centre to another and each centre should have its own veterinary advisor, probably from a local veterinary practice. The veterinary surgeon will know what problems are prevalent in their area and the rehoming centre, and will adjust treatment accordingly. The vaccines that are available are outlined below.

PUPPIES

Vaccinating young puppies is a complex issue. When a bitch whelps, she passes on to her puppies some immunity to any infection to which she is immune. This happens primarily by absorbing antibodies from the first milk the puppy drinks, which is called colostrum. The antibodies are absorbed and pass into the

puppy's bloodstream and these are called maternally derived antibodies (MDA). However, they are then progressively removed by the puppy. The level of MDA halves for about every week of life (actually every 8.3 days, to be accurate!), and so the puppy becomes progressively more susceptible to disease.

This is nature's way of letting the puppy slowly start to stand on his own four feet. However, the MDA will also prevent vaccine working until it sinks to a level where the vaccine can overcome the antibodies. Consequently, it is no good trying to vaccinate very young puppies because it doesn't work.

In practice, the problem is to know when vaccine will work because the level of MDA varies from bitch to bitch, and even between puppies in the same litter. The level of antibody in the blood can be measured, but it is relatively expensive to do and it means taking blood samples from small puppies, which is not easy and can be potentially upsetting for the puppy.

However, we do know the point at which almost all puppies will have a low enough MDA to respond to vaccine and this is the minimum age that vaccine manufacturers use. It varies between vaccines depending on the ability of the vaccine to overcome MDA.

In a rehoming centre the levels of infection to which puppies are exposed is often higher than in a private household. Therefore, many rehoming centres give an initial dose of vaccine before the manufacturer's recommended minimum age to try to ensure that puppies have sufficient immunity to resist any infection that they come across. This may not be a complete course of vaccine, and you should be clear about what vaccines your puppy has received and what has yet to be done. This should be shown on the record of vaccination that you receive when you collect your puppy.

BOOSTERS

It is unlikely that any vaccine will produce a life-long immunity unless there is regular contact with the disease to provoke natural boosters. The vaccination status of dogs entering rehoming centres is often not known, and so most good centres vaccinate dogs on entry to provide the maximum possible protection during their stay.

Once dogs have been rehomed it is necessary to give booster vaccinations to maintain immunity.

There is some controversy about how frequently boosters should be given. Some would argue that too frequent vaccination is dangerous as it may disturb the immune system and so induce immune-mediated diseases. The evidence for this is currently poor, and epidemiology studies have failed to show any link with vaccines used in the United Kingdom. Others argue that the most cost-effective means of maintaining immunity is by giving regular boosters. The best person to advise you about what is appropriate for your dog is your local veterinary surgeon. Only he or she will know the incidence of disease in your local area, and, hence, the potential for your dog being infected or receiving a natural booster. What is certain is that you should consult your veterinary surgeon about a year after the completion of the primary vaccine course or last booster.

It is advisable to discuss boosters with your vet.

DISTEMPER

Distemper and Hardpad are really two forms of the same disease, with Hardpad being the more chronic version of the infection. They are a virus infection that only affects dogs and is likely to be fatal in most cases. The disease usually causes two phases of illness. In the first phase it causes runny eyes (conjunctivitis), sore throat, cough, diarrhoea and vomiting. Dogs usually run a temperature, are off their food and generally listless. The initial phase can last several weeks and can be fatal.

There is then a gap where the dog appears to have fully recovered, but the virus has often affected the brain, causing an encephalitis (infection of the brain). This leads to epileptic fits, which get progressively worse and often end with the dog being euthanased as they become uncontrollable.

All the normal dog vaccines include Distemper as part of the standard vaccination programme.

INFECTIOUS CANINE HEPATITIS

Infectious Canine Hepatitis is caused by Canine Adenovirus 2 (CAV2), and it causes liver disease. The virus is hardy and can live for some time on the ground, so there are often sporadic cases. The symptoms are severe diarrhoea and vomiting coupled with a high temperature and severe abdominal pain, which usually rapidly leads to death in a few hours. Dogs who survive long enough may also show jaundice.

Occasionally, mild cases of disease may cause cloudiness of the cornea (the clear part of the eye) as a result of interaction between the virus and the dog's antibodies. Luckily, Hepatitis is no longer commonly seen.

CANINE PARVOVIRUS

Canine Parvovirus appeared as a new disease worldwide over a period of a few months in the late 70s. The virus is extremely hardy and can survive on the ground for up to two years. Many disinfectants are not effective against the virus, so it is difficult to eliminate.

It may cause different diseases in young puppies compared to older dogs. The virus attacks cells that are dividing, and in young puppies, this includes the muscle of the heart. Therefore, puppies of less than five weeks of age, whose hearts are still growing, can suffer long-term heart failure if they recover from the initial disease.

The primary symptom in all dogs is very severe diarrhoea and vomiting, usually with copious amounts of blood especially in the diarrhoea. The inside lining of the gut, which regrows every 48 hours, is effectively removed, and the number of white blood cells that fight infection drastically reduced. The resultant dehydration and toxicity are often fatal, and there may be 10 per cent mortality, even with high-quality treatment.

LEPTOSPIROSIS

Leptospirosis is a bacterial disease with several different strains. Most strains prefer a particular species, but some can infect several species, including man. The bacterium can be carried by rats, hence it is also known as Rat Borne Jaundice. The disease in humans is called Weil's Disease. The bacteria can readily live in dirty water, such as the bottom of ditches, but will rapidly die once it is dried out, and is relatively easy to kill with disinfectants.

Kennel Cough is highly infectious, and can spread quickly when dogs are kennelled together.

Leptospirosis causes a hepatitis that is similar to Infectious Canine Hepatitis and also inflammation of the kidneys. The symptoms are again severe diarrhoea and vomiting coupled with a high temperature, severe abdominal pain and kidney failure. However, because Leptospirosis is a bacterial disease, it will respond to antibiotics if treated early enough – but rapid diagnosis is obviously very important. Because there is the possibility that humans in contact with the bacteria can also be infected, hygiene is extremely important, and thorough washing of hands after any contact with the dog is essential.

KENNEL COUGH

In contrast to the diseases outlined above, Kennel Cough is not caused by a single agent, and so effective vaccination is a complicated matter. There are a number of agents that may produce the symptoms and these include Para-Influenza 3 (Pi3), which is a virus, and Bordetella Bronchiseptica, which is a bacterium. Vaccines are available for both.

Kennel Cough is technically known as an infectious tracheitis and, as the name suggests, it causes an inflammation in the trachea, or windpipe. The infective agents are carried in droplets in the air, and so infection is much more likely where several dogs are kept in the same building. It is this curious mode of infection that gives the disease its name.

The inflammation causes a severe cough, which is similar to Whooping Cough in children. Dogs are rarely ill, although they may have a slight pus discharge from their noses. Occasionally a secondary pneumonia may develop, and this seems more common in the largest breeds, such as Wolfhounds.

Treatment with antibiotic usually reduces the

cough, but it may well continue for several weeks. While the dog does not usually seem to suffer any ill effects, a heavy cough is not a good recipe for an undisturbed night's sleep for either the dog or the owner. Because of the mode of infection of Kennel Cough, rehoming centres inevitably get the infection fairly often. Many use both Pi3 and Bordetella vaccine when dogs arrive, in order to reduce the incidence, but because of the nature of the disease this is not always successful.

RABIES

Rabies affects all mammals, including dogs and humans. The virus is excreted in saliva, and so a bite from an infected animal is the usual route of infection. Infection leads to an invariably fatal encephalitis (infection of the brain).

There have been only two cases of Rabies in the UK outside quarantine since quarantine was introduced in 1922, and both of those dogs were inadvertently infected while in quarantine because procedures were not properly followed. Consequently, there is no argument for using Rabies vaccine in rehoming centres. If you are thinking of taking your dog abroad, you should consult your veterinary surgeon or the DEFRA website at least eight months before you wish to travel.

The address for the DEFRA website is www.defra.gov.uk/animalh/quarantine/index.htm

WORMING

There are broadly two types of worms that can affect dogs: tapeworms and roundworms. They are quite different, have different lifecycles and need different drugs to treat them.

TAPEWORMS

Tapeworms are relatively uncommon. They are long and thin and are divided into segments. The head, or scolex, is attached to the side of the small intestine, and new segments are continually produced. The oldest segments, each of which contains several million eggs, drop off the body of the worm and are passed in the dog's faeces, or wriggle out of the dog's anus where they may easily be seen.

As the segment dries out, it bursts, and the eggs are released into the environment. If one of those eggs is eaten by the intermediate host, the lifecycle continues, but naturally the chances of this happening are small. The intermediate host can be a flea or some mammals, such as small rodents or even sheep. The intermediate host varies between the different species of tapeworm. Once inside the intermediate host the tapeworm develops into a cyst, which contains a new scolex.

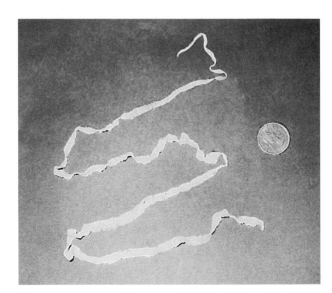

Tapeworm passed by an adult dog (the coin gives an indication of size).

If the intermediate host is eaten by a dog, the scolex is activated by stomach acid, attaches itself to the gut wall and a new tapeworm is born. The new scolex starts to produce segments and the first are shed about six weeks later.

Because of the convoluted lifecycle, tapeworms are not common, and are almost never seen in young puppies. However, rehoming centres often treat for tapeworms when dogs come to the centre with the only 100 per cent effective drug, Praziquantel.

ROUNDWORMS

All dogs have roundworms at some time in their lives. They are long and thin, and vary in length from a few millimetres up to 10 centimetres. There are no specific symptoms of the commonest roundworm, but some more unusual species may cause the dog to rub his bottom on the floor, which is more usually the result, the dog's anal glands being over-full.

Adult dogs have relatively few roundworms, which are irrelevant to the dog. However, those worms continually lay microscopic eggs, which are passed in the faeces. The eggs are potentially infectious to other dogs but, more importantly, they very occasionally infect a human, leading to a disease called visceral larvae migrans. There are a small handful of cases every year in UK, which often get blown out of proportion by the media. Most cases affect young children, and may lead to blindness or inflammation of the brain. It is therefore important that roundworms are controlled even in adult dogs. Routine hygiene measures, such as cleaning up after your dog and ensuring children wash their hands and don't put dirty fingers in their mouths, are

Puppies should be routinely treated for roundworm.

equally important.

The lifecycle is less convoluted than tapeworms. The eggs, laid by worms, are voided in faeces and undergo a short period of maturation before they become infectious. They then remain dormant for many years in the surface layers of the ground. A dog sniffing around may sniff up an infectious egg, which is then swallowed. Once in the gut, the egg hatches to produce a larva. This larva proceeds to burrow through the wall of the gut and up to the lungs via the liver. While this is going on, the larva grows and goes through a number of hatching processes similar to the process that a caterpillar goes through to produce a butterfly. Once in the lungs, the worm is coughed up and swallowed to become a new adult roundworm living in the gut.

Small numbers of roundworms undergoing this process do remarkably little damage to the gut, liver and lungs. In bitches some get stopped along the way and form cysts in the wall of the gut. These worms lie dormant until the bitch becomes pregnant. They are then mobilised and some work their way into the puppies while they are still in the uterus, while others work their way to the mammary glands and are excreted with milk.

Consequently, unless the bitch is treated with some drugs during pregnancy, all puppies are born with roundworms or acquire them in the first few days of life. However, there is a critical difference between puppies and adults because the older dog has some form of immunity that can control the number of worms. Puppies lack such protection and can therefore have very large numbers, often hundreds, of roundworms. The consequence of large numbers of worms migrating through the gut, liver and lungs is highly significant, and may even be severe enough to kill the puppy. More frequently, heavy roundworm burdens lead to a pot-bellied appearance coupled with emaciation.

Luckily there are some very effective drugs to treat roundworms, but there are still some on the market with very poor efficacy, particularly against the immature worms that cause so much damage. A good rehoming centre will treat all their dogs routinely with an effective drug. Puppies should be treated several times in the first few weeks of life, and adult dogs should be regularly treated as well. When you adopt your dog you should be given information on when roundworm treatments have been administered and what drug was used.

The most effective drugs are those that kill both the immature worms as well as the adults, such as Fenbendazole, Mebendazole and Pyrantel. Fenbendazole is the most commonly used. Some other drugs work well against adult roundworms and so are suitable for use only in adult dogs. Nitroscanate and Selamectin are commonly used and the latter is also effective against fleas.

SKIN CONDITIONS

Regular grooming is essential for any dog, and the thicker the coat, the more effort and frequency are required (see Chapter Five).

There are a huge number of diseases that may affect a dog's skin, and so only those of particular relevance to the rehomed dog will be mentioned here. However, we should never forget that the skin is the largest organ of the body and so any disease that causes severe disease will have commensurate effects on the dog.

FLEAS

Fleas are by far the most common skin disease to affect dogs, and they are most likely to be transmitted to humans. Adult fleas will often jump from a dog to their accompanying human, and flea larvae will jump on to anything warm. While fleas in small numbers may not cause a significant problem to most dogs, some have an allergic reaction, which may cause severe disease.

The adult flea is small, brown and flattened, so that it can run quickly between the hairs on the skin. This ability to run rapidly may make them difficult to find. The majority of fleas are found at the base of the tail and in the groin. They feed on the dog's blood, which they obtain by biting through the skin. They produce faeces that is dark brown, as it is digested blood. This may be difficult to find, especially in dogs with a dense coat, such as a collie. To look more closely, stand the dog on a sheet of newspaper and groom for a few minutes. Collect all the bits that have fallen off and look for flea dirt. If there is any doubt whether small black particles are flea dirt, add one to a drop of water. The water will turn red because it is digested blood.

The flea life cycle is remarkably simple. The adults live on the dog and lay eggs, which are slippery, and so quickly fall off the dog as a result of normal activity. The eggs hatch into a larva, which burrows into carpets, bedding or crevices on the ground. There they go through a hatching process, feeding on general dirt in the surroundings until finally they hatch as a new young flea.

This process is temperature dependent, and can take as short a time as two weeks in warm weather. In cold weather, the development process may stop altogether until temperatures rise, so there are inevitably more fleas in the summer and in centrally heated houses in winter. The youngster crawls up to the surface, and, when it detects something warm, will hop towards it. Fleas can hop remarkably high, several hundred times their own body height, and so they soon find a new host (hopefully a dog) for their first meal.

All good rehoming centres put a lot of effort into controlling fleas. Dogs should be routinely treated and, of course, the environment should

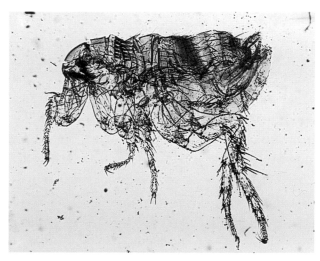

The dog flea – Ctenocephalides canis.

be kept clean. In the house this is done by regular cleaning with a vacuum, and in a kennel environment by regular washing. In addition, it is helpful to use an environmental preparation. The best active ingredient is Methoprene, as it is non-toxic and works by preventing the larvae from hatching to the next stage of the lifecycle. Treatment of the dog is most easily achieved by using one of the modern spot-on products, such as Selamectin, Fipronyl or Imidacloprid.

LICE
The lice that dogs get are very similar to those that so commonly infect children. They are not really a health hazard, but do cause intense irritation and will occasionally crawl on to the dog's owner. They can be difficult to see, but careful examination of the ear flaps and base of the tail will reveal the lice and perhaps the small white eggs glued on to hairs. Fipronyl is the only licensed treatment. Lice are uncommon in well-managed rehoming centres.

TICKS

Ticks can carry diseases – in particular, Lyme Disease, which is relatively common in south-west England. They are not often found on dogs coming from rehoming centres. The ticks are actually intended to live on sheep, but will parasitise any animal. The tick jumps on the dog and buries its mouth in the skin to suck blood. When it first gets on the dog it measures only a few millimetres across and is white. As it becomes engorged with blood over several days, it swells to almost 10 millimetres and changes to a purple colour.

Once the tick is engorged, it drops off naturally and lives on the ground for up to a year, feeding on its blood meal. It then waits until another animal walks past and hops on again for another meal. Before each meal there is a hatching process and eventually an adult emerges, which breeds and dies.

Because the tick's mouth is buried in the skin, it is important never to pull off a tick, as the mouth is likely to snap off and may cause an infection. Tick removal is best left to an expert, such as your veterinary surgeon, who can use a special implement to tease out the mouth. Fipronyl is effective against ticks as well as fleas.

CHEYLETIELLA (RABBIT FUR MITE)

Cheyletiella is primarily a disease of rabbits. As many rehoming centres are in rural settings, there is a risk of infection with this mite from wild rabbits. It lives on the skin but causes intense irritation as it walks around. The mites can sometimes be seen with the naked eye, and usually with a magnifying glass. There is also very obvious dandruff on which the mites feed,

and which may appear to move as the mites crawl around.

The mites will live on any animal, so humans in contact are often affected as the mite crawls off the dog on to them. The fore-arms are the most commonly affected part of the human's body, as the mites crawl on to the hands while the dog is being handled. Fipronyl is usually effective.

RINGWORM

Ringworm is actually caused by a fungus, not a worm. The fungus invades the surface of the skin and hairs causing hair loss. Thankfully, it is rare in dog rehoming centres but can be a real problem with cats. Ringworm is often infectious to humans but almost invariably produces obvious symptoms in dogs (unlike cats). No responsible rehoming centre would rehome a dog with ringworm as it can be difficult to treat both the dog and the human.

INTESTINAL DISEASES

Diarrhoea and vomiting is probably the most common illness that affects dogs in general. Although it may be caused by a specific infectious agent, more often than not it is circumstances that induce an upset stomach. Because the bacteria that inhabit a dog's gut reflect the diet the dog is being given, any sudden change of food is likely to induce diarrhoea. In addition, any circumstance that causes stress will do so as well.

Inevitably where there are large numbers of dogs together, and with a relatively high turnover, the incidence of upset stomachs in dogs in rehoming centres is relatively high.

There are some organisms that are almost normal in rehoming centres, which can also cause diarrhoea and vomiting. If any diarrhoea persists for more than a day or so, or if there is severe vomiting or blood in the faeces, veterinary attention should be sought immediately and, of course, the rehoming centre informed.

Most instances of mild diarrhoea and vomiting can be successfully managed without recourse to expensive treatment. As long as the dog has none of the severe signs mentioned above, simple starvation for 24 hours, with water limited to small quantities hourly, will allow most upset stomachs to settle. As long as the symptoms do not persist, a light diet of white meat, fed little but often, should follow the starvation period for two days. This allows the bacteria to regain their balance. A gradual change back to normal food over five to seven days should then resolve the problem.

Moving from a rehoming centre, itself a stressful environment for a dog, to a new home induces high levels of stress and so it is not surprising that some dogs have diarrhoea as a result. As long as the dog is well in himself, and can keep fluids down, there is no cause for concern. But it is worth taking some simple preventive precautions for the sake of the dog – as well as the kitchen floor covering. Obviously the most important element is to try to reduce the stress of the change to a minimum, and good rehoming centres will encourage the whole family, including other dogs, to get to know your new dog before the move to the new home. Keeping the atmosphere calm, and discouraging visitors, will also help to reduce stress. This stress reduction is at least part of why good rehoming centres do not usually release dogs just before the excitement of Christmas.

Pheromones are substances that are excreted by animals in some circumstances and are specific to each species. They are similar to smells but, although humans cannot smell them, they influence the mood of the dog. Synthetic pheromones are now produced for the dog in a form called dog appeasing pheromone (DAP). In nature this is produced by the mammary area of a bitch and keeps the puppies quiet and calm.

If you are concerned about your dog's health, do not delay in seeking veterinary advice.

The reward of giving a dog a second chance is immeasurable.

The DAP is produced by a diffuser, which is available from veterinary surgeons, and installing one in the area where your new dog will spend most of his time a few days before adoption will also help to reduce stress.

Because of the balance of bacteria mentioned above, good rehoming centres will normally ensure that the same food is given to the dog in the first few days in a new home. This ensures that the balance is maintained. It is also advisable to reduce the total quantity of food for the first day or so and to divide food into several smaller meals.

DENTAL CARE

As dogs age, their teeth tend to cause increasing problems largely because they do not brush them. Of course, this can be prevented if you brush their teeth for them and most dogs can be trained to accept this (see page 60).

Dogs do not generally get the same dental disease that humans get, called caries, from eating sweet foods. They do get plaque on their teeth and that is why brushing helps to prevent problems. If the plaque is not removed, it gradually becomes mineralised and turns into scale. This gradually gets thicker and can get as much as 6 mm on the teeth. Scale inevitably irritates gums, and this often leads to infection, which works down the root of the tooth. The teeth eventually become loose and need removing.

Many rehoming centres will allow dogs to be adopted with some scale on their teeth. As long as there is no sign of gum disease, this is perfectly normal. If you train the dog to have a daily brushing of teeth and also give some things to chew, such as a Kong or hide chew, this will probably halt the progression of the scale and no further attention will be needed. However, you should ask your veterinary surgeon to monitor the state of your dog's teeth to ensure they are not causing any pain.

SUMMING UP

Taking on a rescued dog is a major undertaking, and not to be taken lightly. There may well be initial problems while the dog adapts to his new home and overcomes the traumas he has experienced. However, the dog is a remarkably adaptable animal, and with love, care, training, and lots of patience, he really can make a fresh start – all because you have given him a second chance.